Questions and Answers

Q&A

MODERN WORLD
HISTORY

Greg Lacey   History Officer
Colin Shephard   Chief Examiner

SERIES EDITOR: BOB McDUELL

Letts
EDUCATIONAL

Contents

HOW TO USE THIS BOOK	1
THE IMPORTANCE OF USING QUESTIONS FOR REVISION	2
ASSESSMENT OBJECTIVES IN HISTORY	2
SUMMARY OF ADVICE ON USING SOURCES	5
EXAMINATION TECHNIQUE	5

QUESTIONS AND REVISION SUMMARIES

1	The Peace Treaties of 1919–20 and the League of Nations	6
2	Germany, 1919–39	9
3	Russia, 1917–41	14
4	The United States of America, 1919–41	19
5	Events in the 1930s leading to the Second World War	26
6	The Cold War	28
7	The Soviet invasion of Czechoslovakia, 1968	31
8	Mock examination paper	37

ANSWERS	41

Introduction

HOW TO USE THIS BOOK

The aim of the Questions and Answers series is to provide you with help to do as well as possible in your exams at GCSE level. This book is based on the idea that an experienced Examiner can give, through examination questions, sample answers and advice, the help students need to secure success and improve their grades.

This Questions and Answers series is designed to provide:

- Advice on the different types of question and how to answer them to maximise your marks.
- Information about the skills and types of understanding that will be tested on the examination papers. These are called the **Assessment Objectives**. The Questions and Answers series is intended to help you develop skills and understanding by showing you how marks are allocated.
- Many examples of **examination questions**, arranged by topic. Only try the questions once you have revised a topic thoroughly. It is best not to consult the answers before trying the questions.
- **Sample answers** to all the questions.
- **Advice from Examiners**. By using the experience of Chief Examiners we are able to give advice on how you can improve your answers and avoid the most common mistakes.

To use this book as effectively as possible it is important that you have information on the particular syllabus that you are studying. There are several GCSE Modern World History syllabuses; all have many features in common, but are also different in important respects. They include different choices of topics, and differ in the ways in which these topics are examined. Each of the following Examining Groups has its own Modern World History syllabus:

- Midland Examining Group (MEG)
- Northern Examinations and Assessment Board (NEAB)
- Southern Examining Group (SEG)
- London Examinations
- Welsh Joint Education Committee (WJEC)
- Northern Ireland Council for the Curriculum Examinations and Assessment (NICCEA)

You need to know which of the above syllabuses you are studying, and which topics within the syllabus your teacher has chosen to cover. You will then know which sections of this book you should concentrate on.

This book includes examples of questions on the most popular topics in GCSE Modern World History. It is therefore likely that most, if not all, of the topics you have studied in class will be covered. The material is organised topic by topic, so that as you cover a topic in class, or in your revision, you can refer to the relevant section in this book, gaining valuable experience in practising your historical skills on real questions from previous examinations.

Even though some of the questions will not be taken from the syllabus you are studying, the material will still be of help to you, as the questions in the different Groups' examinations are of similar types, and the **Assessment Objectives** (that is, the knowledge, skills, and historical understanding being tested) are the same. Nevertheless, as good revision technique, you should also obtain copies of past papers for the syllabus you are studying, so that you are familiar with the content, style and layout of the particular papers and questions you will face in the examination.

History is not one of those subjects where, in general, the examiners are just looking for correct factual knowledge. They are concerned with how you *use* your knowledge to construct historical explanations and to deal with historical sources. This book, then, is not intended to teach you the facts about the events you have studied – you can revise these from your class notes and textbooks. Instead, each section of this book will show you how to make the best use of what you already know, in order to do as well as you can in the examination.

Introduction

THE IMPORTANCE OF USING QUESTIONS FOR REVISION

Past examination questions play an important part in revising for examinations. However, don't start practising questions too early. Nothing can be more disheartening than trying to do a question which you do not understand because you have not mastered the topic. So study a topic thoroughly before attempting any questions on it.

How can past examination questions provide a way of preparing for the examination? It is unlikely that any question in this book will appear in exactly the same form on the papers you are going to take. However, the number of totally original questions that can be set on any part of the syllabus is very limited, so similar questions come up over and over again. It will help your confidence if the question you are trying to answer in the examination is familiar and you know you have done similar questions before.

Practising examination questions will highlight gaps in your knowledge and understanding, helping you to identify topics which you need to revise more thoroughly. It will indicate which sorts of questions you can do well. Attempting past questions will also get you used to the type of language used in examinations.

Finally, having access to answers, as you do in this book, will enable you to see clearly what the Examiner thinks is the best way of answering each question.

ASSESSMENT OBJECTIVES IN HISTORY

Assessment objectives are the qualities which are tested in the examination. There are three assessment objectives which are common to all GCSE History syllabuses. The wording of these objectives may vary slightly in the syllabuses of the different Examining Groups but don't worry about this; the objectives are essentially the same.

Objective 1: You should be able to recall, select, organise and deploy knowledge of the subject content.

This is the objective which is concerned with your factual knowledge of the topics you have studied, and your ability to organise and communicate that knowledge. In one sense, this is the most important objective of all, because without any factual knowledge you cannot demonstrate historical understanding, and without the ability to do that you would never persuade the Examiner that you knew anything. Both of the other assessment objectives therefore depend on this one. However, on its own, this objective is not really what GCSE History is all about. Questions testing this objective alone would be concerned solely with the facts; no description, no argument, no analysis, no explanation. There will not be many of them, and they will require you simply to recall information about the events you have studied, but since factual knowledge is bound to be present in answers which relate to the other objectives, there is no real need to test it on its own. Objective 1 is an *enabling* objective – something which helps you to show your ability on the other objectives – rather than an end in itself. You need factual knowledge, and the more detailed and accurate your knowledge the better, but do not expect many questions which test Objective 1 alone.

Objective 2: You should be able to describe, analyse and explain: a) events, changes and issues, and b) the key features and characteristics of the periods, societies and events that you have studied.

The importance of this objective is that it tests your ability to describe, analyse and construct explanations of historical events and developments. In GCSE History examinations you will not often be asked 'What happened....?'. Instead the questions might explore 'Why did it happen?',

Introduction

'What did it change?', 'Why did people react to it in a certain way?' These are not the kinds of questions to which answers will be correct or incorrect, because they involve opinions – your opinions. This does not mean that you can simply write down anything which occurs to you. For your opinions to have any value they must be supported by valid historical examples (which is where your knowledge of the events comes in).

Objective 2 questions will often involve certain concepts like continuity and change, or cause and consequence, around which historical explanations of events and issues are constructed. Questions in the examination may target one or other of these concepts to test the level of understanding you can demonstrate in your answer. Let's take the example of the Treaty of Versailles to show some of the different types of question which can test Objective 2. For example:

- In what ways was Germany punished by the Treaty of Versailles? (*description*)
- Why did the Allies make a harsh treaty with Germany? (*explanation of causes*)
- How successful was the Treaty of Versailles? (*analysis of consequences*)
- Was Germany still a great power after 1919? (*analysis of continuity/change*)

In answering each of these questions you would have to describe, analyse and explain events. Later in this book you will find many examples of how to do this. Here it is enough to say that it matters much less what your explanation is, than how you go about constructing it. The Examiner has no single right answer in mind; what counts is the quality of thought that goes into your answer, and your ability to support thoughts with accurate and relevant historical examples.

An important aspect of analysing and explaining the key features and characteristics of societies you have studied is showing you understand the thoughts, motives and beliefs of people who lived in the past; that is, being able to view historical events from the perspective of people alive at the time. In explaining why something happened, it can often be relevant to include mention of the motives or beliefs of those involved in the events. In explaining why a development was important, its impact on the ways of life of the people affected by it can be significant.

Objective 3: In relation to the subject content you have studied, you should be able: a) to comprehend, interpret, evaluate and use a range of sources of information of different types, and b) to comprehend, interpret and evaluate representations and interpretations of events, people and issues.

You will notice that this objective has two elements, dealing first with sources and second with interpretations and representations. Sources are the 'raw materials' from which historians can find out about the past: documents, pictures, accounts, placenames, artefacts, and so on. Representations and interpretations are created when people try to reconstruct the past; this could be an historian writing about an event, a witness trying to remember what she had seen, or an artist drawing a picture of an event in the past. In practice, there is no clear dividing line between what counts as a source and what counts as an interpretation (in fact, most people would agree that all interpretations are themselves sources), and you certainly do not need to worry about the difference between them. In the examination you will be asked to deal with a range of sources of different types, and some of these will doubtless be interpretations. You can apply the same skills you have learnt during the course to sources and interpretations alike.

Sources will be used in all the examination papers, but in different ways. Watch out for 'stimulus material' questions. These include sources, but only to give you information to use in your answer. You are not required to interpret or evaluate the stimulus material. Such questions are used to test Objectives 1 and 2, but not Objective 3. If you aren't sure whether or not a question is targeting Objective 3, just ask yourself, 'Could I answer this question without using the source at all?' If the answer is 'Yes', then it is not an Objective 3 question. However, most of the time when sources are included in the questions, the approach is very different. Here Objective 3 will be tested; that is, the questions will require you to interpret and evaluate the sources you are given.

What is the difference between *interpreting* and *evaluating* a source? Interpretation is the process of understanding what a source tells you. This might not be immediately obvious. Take the

Introduction

following telegram sent by the British Prime Minister, Lloyd George, to Field Marshal Haig, British Commander-in-Chief in France, on 16 October, 1917:

> *'The War Cabinet desires to congratulate you upon the achievements of the British armies in the great battle which has been raging since 31st July... You and your men have driven the enemy back with skill and courage and have filled the enemy with alarm. I am personally glad to pass this message to you, and to your gallant troops, and to state again my confidence in your leadership.'*

If asked what this source tells us about progress made by British armies in the 3rd Battle of Ypres during the First World War, we might jump to the conclusion that they were doing well. If we just believed what the source says, or if we knew nothing about this topic, we would not realise that it refers to an offensive which became impossibly bogged down in the mud of Flanders, achieved almost nothing and saw the deaths of around half a million men (of whom, approximately, half were British). To interpret this source, then, we have to use our knowledge of the topic, which will lead us to realise that during wartime the Prime Minister must support the country's armed forces, and cannot afford openly to admit that things are going badly. In this light, the source is not a literal statement of the truth, but an official message of encouragement and support. Interpretation is all about understanding the real *meaning* of a source, and not just taking what it says at face value.

Evaluation takes the process of interpretation a stage further, by asking what use we can make of a source in finding out about the past. So the above source is not much use at all as evidence about the progress of the 3rd Battle of Ypres, in fact it is positively misleading for that purpose, but it could be much more useful as evidence of how British politicians tried to hide the reality of war in order to maintain morale.

Questions on Objective 3 can be very varied in type. The following is a list of skills you might be expected to demonstrate:

1. comprehension of sources
2. location and extraction of relevant information from the sources
3. distinguishing between fact and opinions
4. indicating deficiencies in sources, such as gaps and inconsistencies
5. detecting bias
6. comparing and contrasting sources
7. reaching conclusions based on the use of sources as evidence
8. comparing interpretations of an event
9. explaining how and why interpretations are created

You will find examples of questions testing most of these in this book, along with detailed advice on how to answer them. But remember, when answering Objective 3 questions, *never* judge a source solely by its type – whether a photograph, a cartoon, an eye-witness account, a newspaper article etc. **Always** look at what the source actually tells you and consider its reliability in relation to your knowledge of the topic and the information you already have from other sources. The weakest answers to Objective 3 questions are always those which rely on generalisations, e.g. 'He was an eye-witness, so he must know what happened', or 'Primary sources are more reliable than secondary sources', and ignore what the source itself actually says or shows.

Introduction

SUMMARY OF ADVICE ON USING SOURCES

The following five simple rules should help you to improve your answers to almost all source-based questions:

❶ Never be satisfied with judging the reliability or usefulness of a source by its **type**.

❷ Always use the **content** of a source in your answer.

❸ Do not take sources at face value. Look beneath the surface of the source to what you can infer from it – think about what the source really means, rather than just what it says.

❹ Do not automatically believe a source; always try to **check** what it says. An easy way to start checking is to ask whether any of the other sources you have says the same things. This is called **cross-reference**.

❺ Always use your **knowledge of the topic** to help you judge the reliability or usefulness of a source – in the light of what you know about the topic, can you believe the source or not?

EXAMINATION TECHNIQUE

No book, however useful, will enable you to achieve a high grade if you have poor examination technique. In every examination you take, keep the following pieces of advice in mind:

❶ Read the questions carefully. Where there is a choice of questions, make sure you have read all the questions you could answer, and that you have chosen those you can answer best.

❷ Answer the right number of questions, and complete each question. Obey all the instructions to candidates, such as answering specific numbers of questions from different sections of the paper.

❸ Manage the time you have available effectively. Split the time sensibly between the questions you have to answer. There is little point in writing an enormous amount on a topic you know well, only to fail to complete your last question. All the marks available on questions you do not answer are marks lost to you, so finish the examination, even if it means cutting some answers shorter than you might wish.

❹ The question paper shows how many marks are available on each question. Use this as a guide to the amount of time to spend on each question. Do not write lengthy answers to questions which carry few marks.

❺ Answer the question as it is asked, and not how you might wish it to be. The most common fault in examination technique is irrelevance. Marks are only given for answers that do what the question asks.

❻ In History examinations you are expected to produce ideas, arguments, explanations. It is important to support these with relevant examples. Never make unsupported assertions.

❼ Remember that marks will be awarded for accurate spelling, punctuation and grammar. Check through your work carefully at the end of the examination and correct any errors.

1 The Peace Treaties of 1919–20 and the League of Nations

REVISION SUMMARY

1 INTRODUCTION

- On 11 November 1918 the First World War came to an end.
- The Great Powers on the victorious side – Britain, France, Italy and the United States – had to decide how the losers would be treated.
- Many people in the victorious countries wanted to take revenge on the losers.
- The cost of the war, both human and material, was huge. Around eight and a half million people were killed in the fighting. Many countries were almost bankrupted after the war.
- Even before the end of fighting, great changes were taking place in many countries. The Austro-Hungarian empire was disintegrating, as was the Ottoman (Turkish) empire. The Bolshevik Revolution in November 1917 took Russia into a period of civil war. In Germany itself the Kaiser abdicated in November 1918, and the country seemed on the brink of revolution.
- In January 1919 representatives of the victorious powers met in Paris to decide on the terms of the peace settlement. The major decisions were taken by Lloyd George and Clemenceau, the Prime Ministers of Britain and France, and President Wilson of the United States.
- In 1919–20 treaties between the victors and each of the defeated nations were signed:

   Treaty of Versailles (1919) with Germany
   Treaty of St Germain (1919) with Austria
   Treaty of Neuilly (1919) with Bulgaria
   Treaty of Trianon (1920) with Hungary
   Treaty of Sèvres (1920) with Turkey, later amended by the Treaty of Lausanne (1923)

2 THE TREATY OF VERSAILLES

- The French wanted Germany weakened so that it would never again be a threat to France. The British and Americans had doubts about this, but in the end agreed to punish Germany. The Germans were given no choice but to sign the treaty; they were not allowed to join in the negotiations.
- Germany lost territory in Europe, and had all its colonies taken away. The League of Nations took over the Saar and Danzig.
- The size of Germany's armed forces was strictly limited.
- Germany had to accept responsibility for the war ('war guilt') and agree to pay reparations.
- The Rhineland was demilitarised.
- The Treaty of Brest-Litovsk with Russia was made void, which enabled Poland, Estonia, Latvia and Lithuania to become independent states. Poland was given access to the Baltic Sea through the 'Polish Corridor'.
- The League of Nations was established.
- The treaty left many Germans feeling resentful at the treatment their country had received. Many non-Germans felt that it was foolish to treat Germany so harshly.

3 THE OTHER PEACE TREATIES

- The Austro-Hungarian empire was broken up, and new states established (Czechoslovakia, Austria, Hungary, Yugoslavia).
- *Anschluss* (union between Austria and Germany) was forbidden.
- Italy and Rumania received territory from the old Austro-Hungarian empire.
- Bulgaria lost territory to Yugoslavia and Greece.
- The Ottoman empire was broken up, with much of it being taken as League of Nations mandates.

The Peace Treaties of 1919–20 and the League of Nations

REVISION SUMMARY

4 THE LEAGUE OF NATIONS

- The idea of an international organisation to preserve world peace was included as one of President Wilson's '14 Points', the principles he had stated as a framework for ending the First World War.
- The League was established in the peace treaties of 1919–20. It was based in Geneva, Switzerland.
- The League consisted of the following organisations:
  1. The **Assembly** – all member states were represented in the Assembly, which discussed matters of international importance. Because all members had an equal vote, the Assembly did not have much power. The Great Powers dominated the League by being permanent members of the Council.
  2. The **Council** – this met more frequently than the Assembly, and was intended to cope with crises as they arose. Britain, France, Italy and Japan were permanent members. The Assembly voted for additional non-permanent members.
  3. The **Permanent Court of Justice** – this dealt with legal disputes between member states.
  4. The **Agencies** – the League set up a number of commissions to deal with a range of international problems such as mandates, health, refugees and labour.

5 WEAKNESSES OF THE LEAGUE

- Not all nations were members of the League. The USA was never a member, and of the Great Powers, only Britain and France were members throughout the life of the League.
- The League lacked the power to enforce its decisions. It had no army and relied on 'collective security' against aggressors. In practice, it could be ignored by powerful nations.
- As early as 1923, over the Corfu Incident, the League showed itself incapable of dealing with acts of aggression.
- The first major crisis for the League occurred when the Japanese invaded Manchuria in 1931. The League condemned Japan, but Japan simply withdrew from the League. Japanese aggression against China continued.
- The Italian invasion of Ethiopia was a disaster for the League. Although Italy was condemned and some sanctions put on it, the League failed to place sanctions on oil, which would have had some effect. Britain and France failed to give the League proper support. The League was powerless to prevent Italy completing the conquest of Ethiopia.

6 ACHIEVEMENTS OF THE LEAGUE

- The commissions of the League did much useful work.
- The League was successful in resolving some international disputes, e.g. the Aaland Islands dispute between Sweden and Finland, and the Greek attack on Bulgaria in 1925.
- During the 1920s membership of the League increased, notably with the inclusion of Germany from 1926.
- The League's existence gave opportunities for disputes to be solved by discussion rather than force.

If you need to revise this subject more thoroughly, see the relevant topics in the *Letts GCSE World History Study Guide*.

1 The Peace Treaties of 1919–20 and the League of Nations

QUESTIONS

1 Study the source carefully, and then answer the questions which follow.

SOURCE A

A British cartoon of 1920 about the League of Nations.

THE GAP IN THE BRIDGE.

(a) Look at Source A

What is the cartoonist saying about the League of Nations? Explain your answer, referring to details in the cartoon. (5)

(b) What did the Great Powers want to achieve when they set up the League of Nations? (5)

MEG specimen 1998

2 (a) What limits did the Treaty of Versailles place on Germany's military strength? (4)

(b) Why did the victorious powers want to limit Germany's strength? (6)

(c) 'The most important reason why Germany hated the Treaty of Versailles was the military restrictions.' Do you agree with this statement? Explain your answer. (10)

MEG specimen 1998

Germany, 1919–39

2

This chapter deals only with events inside Germany. It does not cover foreign policy.

REVISION SUMMARY

1 THE ESTABLISHMENT OF THE WEIMAR REPUBLIC

- By October 1918 it was clear that Germany would lose the First World War and would soon have to make peace.
- By the beginning of November, sailors and soldiers began to mutiny. There were calls for Kaiser William II to abdicate. Germany was on the brink of revolution.
- On 9 November, the Kaiser abdicated and the Republic was declared. On 11 November the armistice with the Allies was signed, and the war came to an end.
- These developments did not bring stability within Germany. Left-wing groups like the Spartacists tried to start a Communist revolution. They were crushed by the army and the *Freikorps* in January 1919.
- In January 1919 elections were held, and in February the National Assembly met in the town of Weimar (hence the 'Weimar Republic'). The Assembly produced a new constitution for Germany. Friedrich Ebert, leader of the Social Democrats (who had taken over the government on the Kaiser's abdication), became the first President of the Republic.

2 THE WEIMAR REPUBLIC

- The Republic survived until 1933. It faced many problems, but also had many successes.
- Many Germans blamed the Republic for the country's failure to win the First World War. They believed that Germany had not been defeated on the battlefield but had been 'stabbed in the back' by the politicians who signed the armistice. The Republic was also blamed for what Germans saw as the harsh terms of the Treaty of Versailles.
- There were a number of revolts by right-wing groups. The most famous of these was the Munich *Putsch* in 1923 led by Adolf Hitler. It was put down by the police and Hitler was sent to prison.
- The main problems faced by the Republic were economic. As a result of the Treaty of Versailles, Germany was faced with a bill of £6,600 million to be paid in instalments. Germany fell behind with the payments, following which France sent troops in 1923 to occupy the Ruhr, Germany's main coal and steel area. The government tried to make up for the lost production by printing money. This led to inflation. Soon the German mark was worthless.
- The economic recovery was led by Gustav Stresemann, who was Chancellor in 1923 and Foreign Minister until his death in 1929. In 1923 a new currency, called the Rentenmark, was introduced. The Dawes Plan of 1924 also helped. By this the Allies allowed Germany to pay the reparations in easier stages, and arranged for the withdrawal of French troops from the Ruhr. The USA lent Germany nearly $800 million. This money was invested in German industries which prospered. More goods were produced and unemployment fell.

3 THE DEPRESSION AND THE RISE OF HITLER

- Between 1924 and 1929 the Republic was a success. Most Germans accepted it and extremist parties such as Hitler's National Socialist (Nazi) party had little support.
- In 1929 the Wall Street stock market crashed. US investments in Germany were withdrawn. Many companies went bankrupt and by 1932, 6 million Germans were unemployed.
- In this atmosphere of depression and poverty Hitler's National Socialist party increased its support. Since the failure of the *putsch* in 1923 and his release from prison the following year, Hitler had decided to use lawful means to gain power. In the elections in 1930 and 1932 Hitler attacked the economic and foreign policies of the Republic. He promised to cut the numbers of unemployed and to make Germany great again.

2 Germany, 1919–39

REVISION SUMMARY

- In the July 1932 elections the Nazis became the largest single party in the Reichstag, but they did not have an overall majority. In the November elections the Nazis lost some support but remained the largest party. President Hindenburg and his advisers thought that if Hitler was appointed Chancellor they would be able to control him. So on 30 January 1933 Hitler became Chancellor of a government of which there were only three Nazi members. He immediately demanded a new election.

4 HITLER BECOMES A DICTATOR

- In another election in March 1933 the Nazis still failed to win an overall majority, despite the SA and SS intimidating their opponents. Hitler now used intimidation to force the Reichstag to pass the Enabling Act. This allowed him to make laws without the consent of the Reichstag.
- The SA and the SS arrested political opponents, many of whom were sent to concentration camps. In July 1933 all political parties, except the Nazi Party, were banned. When Hindenburg died in 1934, Hitler gave himself a new title, *Führer* (leader).

5 LIFE IN NAZI GERMANY

- **Propaganda**. The Nazis kept control over the German people partly by terror. The Gestapo (secret state police) and the SS hunted down and removed Hitler's opponents. Joseph Goebbels, Minister of Propaganda, used the radio, the cinema and the press to spread Nazi ideas. Strict censorship made sure that opposing views were not seen or heard. Mass rallies were held.
- **Young people** were encouraged to join Nazi youth movements. Education was closely controlled. Girls were to be prepared for motherhood, while boys were to be ready to fight. They were taught that they were members of a master race and were encouraged to hate and despise Jews.
- **The Jews**. Hitler and many Germans believed that the Jews were responsible for many of Germany's troubles. Hitler regarded them as an inferior race, barely human. He thought they would corrupt the purity of the German race. In 1935 the Nuremberg Laws banned marriages between Jews and Germans. Jews also lost their German citizenship and their right to vote. In November 1938 during *Kristallnacht* (Crystal Night), thousands of Jewish shops were smashed and synagogues burned down; 40,000 Jews were rounded up and sent to concentration camps. Between 1941 and 1945 the Germans carried out the 'Final Solution' and murdered 6 million Jews in extermination camps, such as Auschwitz.
- **The German economy** was transformed by the Nazis. In 1936 they introduced the Four-year Plan. This included massive rearmament. Germany also aimed to become self-sufficient in essential raw materials, such as oil. The standard of living of the German people rose. The number of unemployed fell, wages rose and Germans began to be able to afford consumer goods, such as cars. Large public works projects, such as the building of new motorways, provided some of the new jobs, but most were provided in factories making armaments.

If you need to revise this subject more thoroughly, see the relevant topics in the Letts GCSE World History Study Guide.

Germany, 1919–39

1 (a) During 1923 the Weimar Republic was threatened by these events:

   (i) the French invasion of the Ruhr;

   (ii) the inflation of the mark;

   (iii) the Beer-Hall Putsch.

     Describe any one of these events. (4)

(b) Why was the Weimar Republic able to survive the events of 1923? (6)

(c) Did the events of 1923 make the Weimar Republic weaker or stronger? Explain your answer. (10)

MEG specimen 1998

2 Study the sources below and then answer the questions which follow.

SOURCE A

> **Extracts from the Nazi Party Programme, 1920.**
>
> 1 We demand the union of all Germans on the basis of the right of self-determination of peoples to form a great Germany.
>
> 2 We demand the abolition of the Treaty of Versailles.
>
> 3 We demand land for settling our surplus population.
>
> 4 Only those of German blood may be a member of the German nation.

SOURCE B

> **Albert Speer, a leading Nazi, recalls what he felt after hearing a speech by Hitler in 1931. From Speer's book written after World War Two.**
>
> Here it seemed to me was hope. Hitler persuaded us that the evils of Communism could be halted. Instead of hopeless unemployment, Germany could move towards economic recovery. It must have been during these months that my mother saw a Storm Trooper parade in the streets of Heidelberg. The sight of discipline in a time of chaos, the impression of energy in an atmosphere of hopelessness, seems to have won her over also.

2 Germany, 1919–39

QUESTIONS

SOURCE C

A Nazi Party poster of 1932. It says 'Our Last Hope: Hitler'.

Unsere letzte Hoffnung: HITLER

SOURCE D

February 27th 1933	Fire breaks out in the Reichstag Building
March 6th 1933	Germans vote in general election
March 23rd 1933	Reichstag passes the Enabling Law

(a) Source A gives four extracts from the Nazi Party Programme of 1920. Use your own knowledge to explain why these were likely to win support for the Nazi Party. (5)

(b) Study Source B

(i) What evidence is there in the source to suggest that it might not be reliable to an historian writing about why Hitler won support before 1933? (3)

Germany, 1919–39

(ii) Use your own knowledge to explain what parts of Source B can be accepted as accurate by an historian writing about why Hitler won support before 1933. (3)

(c) Study Source C.

(i) Why might Source C be useful as evidence to explain why the Nazis became the largest party in the Reichstag in 1933? (3)

(ii) Use your own knowledge to say whether the source fully explains why the Nazis became the largest party in the Reichstag in 1932. (3)

(d) Study Source D.

'The events of February and March 1933 allowed Hitler and the Nazis to take full control of Germany by August 1934.' Use **your own knowledge** to explain whether you agree or disagree with this statement. (8)

(e) EITHER

(i) Why was Germany hit by depression in 1929? Why was the Weimar Republic unable to deal with it? (15)

OR

(ii) What measures did Hitler take between 1934 and 1939 to bring employment to the German people? How successful was he? (15)

NEAB specimen 1998

3 By 1939 the Nazis had been in power in Germany for six years.

Were German working people better off in 1939 than they had been in 1933? Explain your answer. (12)

SEG specimen 1998

3 Russia, 1917–41

REVISION SUMMARY

This chapter deals only with events inside Russia (known from 1923 onwards as the Soviet Union). It does not deal with foreign policy.

1 INTRODUCTION

- From 1894 Russia was ruled by Tsar Nicholas II, who was weak and ineffective.
- Russia was an autocracy – a country in which the Tsar was absolute ruler and the people had little freedom.
- Russia was a poor country. By the early twentieth century industry was beginning to develop, but living conditions in the towns were very bad and in the countryside few of the peasants owned their own land.
- Opposition to the Tsar was growing. Many revolutionary groups wanted to overthrow the Tsar. More moderate opponents wanted social and political reform.
- Defeat in the war against Japan (1904–5) sparked off the 1905 revolution in Russia. The Tsar survived this, but had to grant some reforms, including allowing the Duma (a parliament which had little power) to meet.
- By the outbreak of the First World War in 1914 none of Russia's problems had been solved. Russia joined in the war on the Allied side against Germany.

2 RUSSIA AND THE EFFECTS OF THE FIRST WORLD WAR BY 1917

- By early 1917 Russia's armies were near to defeat.
- The war effort caused great hardship for the civilian population of Russia.
- Tsar Nicholas II was losing control of events, particularly in Petrograd where food riots and strikes broke out.
- The Tsar was unpopular for refusing much needed reforms and because of the influence of his wife and favourites such as Rasputin (murdered in December 1916).

3 THE REVOLUTIONS OF 1917

Note: because of the old calendar in use in Russia at the time, the Revolutions of 1917 can be called either the February/October or the March/November Revolutions.

- The March Revolution led to the abdication of the Tsar.
- The Provisional Government took over, with Kerensky later emerging as leader.
- Also powerful were the 'Soviets', soldiers' and workers' councils, set up in many big cities.
- The Provisional Government stayed in the war and more defeats followed.
- Dissatisfaction with the Provisional Government grew. Revolutionaries, such as the Mensheviks and the Bolsheviks (led by Lenin), increased their influence in the Soviets and planned another revolution.
- In early November, the Bolsheviks' Red Guards seized power in Petrograd. Lenin claimed to be ruler of Russia; in fact, at first the Bolsheviks controlled only a few major cities.

Russia, 1917–41   3

REVISION SUMMARY

4 THE CIVIL WAR AND THE BOLSHEVIK CONSOLIDATION OF POWER, 1918–21

- Lenin had promised 'Peace, bread and land' to the Russian people.
- Peace was made with the Germans by the Treaty of Brest-Litovsk.
- The Bolsheviks introduced Communist rule and set about crushing all opposition.
- Civil War soon broke out. The 'Whites' (opponents of the Bolsheviks) fought against the Red Army, created by Trotsky. Foreign countries helped the Whites, but opposition to the Bolsheviks was never united.
- Lenin used War Communism to ensure the victory of the Red Army by 1921.
- In 1921 the Kronstadt Rising showed Lenin the dangers of continuing with War Communism. He introduced the New Economic Policy (NEP) to allow Russia to recover.

5 STALIN'S RISE TO POWER

- In 1924 Lenin died. Trotsky and Stalin were his two possible successors.
- Trotsky, despite his fame and achievements, was disliked by the other Bolshevik leaders.
- Gradually Stalin, using the power built up in his time as Secretary of the Communist Party, increased his control.
- Trotsky was exiled in 1929. By then, Stalin had emerged as the new leader. Trotsky was eventually murdered, on Stalin's orders, in 1940.

6 STALIN'S RUSSIA

- Stalin proved to be a cruel and ruthless dictator, who transformed Russia into a modern state.
- He abolished the NEP and the state took control of all industry and agriculture.
- The first Five-Year Plan was introduced in 1928. This set production targets for heavy industry. Every five years a new plan set fresh targets. By the outbreak of war in 1941, Russia was a major industrial nation.
- In agriculture, the peasants were forced to work on huge new collective farms. Many peasants, particularly the better-off (called kulaks), resisted this change. Stalin crushed this resistance by force. Production in agriculture was slow to recover.
- Stalin destroyed all opposition. Throughout the 1930s his 'purges' led to the arrest, imprisonment and murder of millions of people, including most political and military leaders.

If you need to revise this subject more thoroughly, see the relevant topics in the Letts GCSE World History Study Guide.

3 Russia, 1917–41

QUESTIONS 1   This question is about the fall of the Tsar. Look carefully at Sources A to F and then answer questions (a) to (e) which follow.

SOURCE A

An extract from the Tsarina's diary, 28 February 1917.

This is a hooligan movement. Young people run and shout that there is no bread simply to create excitement, along with workers who prevent others from working. If the weather were very cold they would probably all stay at home. But this will all pass and calm down if only the Duma will behave itself.

SOURCE B

Rodzianko, President of the Duma, writing about events in Petrograd, 11 March 1917.

Unexpectedly for all, there erupted a soldier mutiny such as I have never seen. These were not soldiers, of course, but peasants taken directly from the plough who have found it useful now to make known their peasant demands. In the crowd, all one could hear was 'Land and Freedom', 'Down with the Dynasty', 'Down with the Romanovs', 'Down with the Officers'.

SOURCE C

Estimates of the numbers of workers on strike in Petrograd in 1917. These were compiled by historians in the late 1980s.

6 March	20,000
7 March	30,000
10 March	250,000
12 March	350,000

SOURCE D

From the diary of a British nurse who was working in Petrograd in 1917.

Sunday, 11 March 1917

A glorious sunny day: at about 3 p.m. I went to the window to look out. There were people on the bridge laughing and talking. I suddenly saw soldiers fire a volley into them. About seven people were hit.

That was that: soldiers had fired on people. Nothing now could stop the revolution.

Russia, 1917–41

SOURCE E

A photograph showing Cossacks joining demonstrators. It was taken in Petrograd in March 1917. The banner reads 'Down with the Tsar: Long live the Republic'.

SOURCE F

(i) A telegram from Michael Rodzianko, the President of the Duma, to Tsar Nicholas II, who was commanding troops on the Eastern Front, dated 11 March 1917.

The situation in Petrograd is serious. The government can do nothing. Food and fuel running out. Troops are firing at each other. Someone who is trusted by the country must be allowed to form a new government.

(ii) A letter from the Tsar Nicholas II to a loyal member of the Duma, 12 March 1917.

That fat Rodzianko has sent me some nonsense. I shall not even reply.

3 Russia, 1917–41

QUESTIONS

(a) Study Source A. What can you learn from Source A about the situation in Petrograd in March 1917? (4)

(b) Study Sources A and B. Source B shows a different attitude to events in Petrograd to that shown in Source A. Use the sources, and your own knowledge, to explain the differences. (6)

(c) Study Sources A, B, C and D. Does the evidence of Sources C and D support the version of events given in Source A or in Source B? Explain your answer. (4)

(d) Study Sources A, B, C, D, E and F. On 15 March 1917, Tsar Nicholas II abdicated. Use the sources, and your own knowledge, to explain why he did this. (6)

(e) 'Nicholas II was responsible for his own downfall.' Use the sources, and your own knowledge, to explain whether or not you agree with this interpretation of the events of March 1917. (10)

Edexcel specimen 1998

2   In November 1917 the Bolsheviks seized power. In the elections which followed the Bolsheviks gained only about a quarter of the votes.

Why, then, were the Bolsheviks still in power by the end of 1921? (12)

SEG specimen 1998

3   (a) What changes did Stalin introduce in agriculture? (4)

(b) Why did he make these changes in agriculture? (6)

(c) Stalin made changes both in industry and in agriculture. Which were the more important – the industrial or the agricultural changes? Explain your answer. (10)

MEG specimen 1998

The United States of America, 1919–41

4

This chapter deals only with events inside the USA. It does not cover foreign policy.

REVISION SUMMARY

1 THE AMERICAN ECONOMY IN THE 1920s

- During the 1920s American industry experienced a 'boom', as production expanded rapidly.
- Consumer goods, such as radios, washing machines and cars, were produced in huge quantities, so that what had once been luxuries now became available to everybody.
- New ideas like hire purchase were used to encourage people to buy consumer goods.
- The US government believed in 'free enterprise', and involved itself as little as possible in the economy.
- Americans enjoyed the highest standard of living in the world.
- However, there were some economic problems. Agriculture was in trouble; overproduction and low prices were driving farmers out of business. By the late 1920s production in industry was slowing down, as the USA found it hard to sell its goods overseas.

2 AMERICAN SOCIETY IN THE 1920s AND 1930s

- The prosperity of the 1920s meant people had time and money for entertainment. Hollywood became the most important centre in the world for film production. Millions of people went to the cinema every week.
- The 'Roaring Twenties' saw great changes in social attitudes and fashions, particularly in the cities.
- In 1920 prohibition was introduced. This made the manufacture and sale of alcohol illegal. Gangsters took over the trade in alcohol, making enormous profits. The main effect of prohibition was to increase crime, and it was eventually repealed in 1933.
- Racism was a feature of American society, particularly in the south. The Ku Klux Klan flourished during these years.

3 THE WALL STREET CRASH AND THE GREAT DEPRESSION

- In October 1929 the New York Stock Exchange, known as 'Wall Street' because of its location, collapsed. The value of shares plunged to a fraction of their previous value. Shareholders were bankrupted.
- The crash was caused by many factors:
  1. Share prices rose too fast, and many people borrowed money to buy them. When the price started to go down, people panicked.
  2. Share prices did not reflect the true condition of the US economy.
  3. The US economy was in trouble before the crash; there was overproduction and unemployment was rising.
  4. The 'boom' had been financed by debt. This was all right while the economy expanded, but a disaster once people could not repay what they owed.
- The crash led to the Great Depression. Investment in industry slumped, unemployment increased, people had no money to spend. By 1932, 12 million people were out of work in the United States.
- The Depression spread to other countries, which led to a fall in international trade. Countries including the USA put higher tariffs (taxes) on imported goods in an attempt to protect jobs in their own industries. These tariffs just reduced trade still further.
- The government of President Hoover had little idea how to cope with the Depression. Like other Republicans, he believed in free enterprise, not in government interference in the economy.
- In the Presidential election of 1932, a Democrat, Franklin Roosevelt, was elected.

4 The United States of America, 1919–41

REVISION SUMMARY

4 THE NEW DEAL

- Roosevelt promised a 'New Deal' to the American people. By this he meant that his government would take whatever steps were necessary to deal with the Depression.

- In his first 'hundred days' in office, Roosevelt dealt with the most urgent problems, in particular by closing down all the weakest banks and providing emergency relief for the unemployed. During this period prohibition was repealed.

- The first New Deal (1933–5) aimed to solve America's unemployment crisis. A series of acts brought into being the 'Alphabetic Agencies', e.g.

  Civilian Conservation Corps (CCC)
  Works Progress Administration (WPA)
  Tennessee Valley Authority (TVA)
  National Recovery Administration (NRA)
  Home Owners Loan Corporation (HOLC).

  The Agricultural Adjustment Act helped farmers by forcing them to accept quotas which reduced overproduction. This helped prices recover.

- The second New Deal after 1935 dealt more with social issues, notably the Social Security Act (1935) which provided pensions and unemployment insurance.

- The New Deal had opponents, particularly among Republicans and rich businessmen who objected to government interference in private enterprise. The Supreme Court declared many of Roosevelt's plans illegal.

- Whether or not the New Deal was a success is difficult to say. Unemployment was reduced from a peak of nearly 13 million in 1933 to under 8 million in 1937, but it was only the Second World War which brought back full employment to the United States.

If you need to revise this subject more thoroughly, see the relevant topics in the Letts GCSE World History Study Guide.

The United States of America, 1919–41

QUESTIONS

1 This question is about the US economy in the 1920s and the Wall Street Crash. Look carefully at Sources A to F and then answer questions (a) to (e) which follow.

SOURCE A

From a speech by President Hoover, 1928.

'We in the USA are nearer the final triumph over poverty than ever before in the history of mankind. During the eight years of rule we have built more homes, built more skyscrapers, done more to increase production and expand export markets than in any previous period.'

SOURCE B

From a history book about the USA, written in 1984.

The prosperity was not shared by everyone. Farmers had never shared in the 1920s boom. Black Americans did not share in the boom either. The fact was that the gap between rich and poor was very large: the top 5% of Americans earned one-third of all the income.

SOURCE C

A table showing the increase in the production of some goods in the USA, 1920–29.

	1920	1929
Motor Cars	9 million	26 million
Telephones	13 million	20 million
Radios	600 000	10 million

SOURCE D

A photograph of the main street of a Californian town in the 1920s.

4 The United States of America, 1919–41

QUESTIONS

SOURCE E

Newspaper headlines, 24 October 1929.

> NEW YORK, THURSDAY, OCTOBER 24, 1929.
>
> ## PRICES OF STOCKS CRASH IN HEAVY LIQUIDATION, TOTAL DROP OF BILLIONS
>
> PAPER LOSS $4,000,000,000
>
> But no Brokerage House is in Difficulties, as Margins have Been Kept High.
>
> 2,600,000 Shares Sold in the Final Hour in Record Decline
>
> ORGANIZED BACKING ABSENT
>
> MANY ACCOUNTS WIPED OUT
>
> Bankers Confer on Steps to Support Market -- Highest Break is 96 Points.

SOURCE F

> **From a British historian writing in 1975 about the reasons for the Wall Street Crash.**
>
> By 1929 it was clear that US industry was making goods faster than it could sell them and that profits were falling. Cautious people began to sell their shares. The panic spread: more and more people realised that their shares were worth a lot only if someone was willing to pay for them. They began to turn their shares into cash. On 29 October 1929, thirteen million shares were sold on the Wall Street Stock Exchange.

(a) Study Source A.
   What can you learn from Source A about the state of the US economy in 1928? (4)

(b) Study Sources A and B.
   Source B shows a different view of the situation in the US to that in Source A.
   Use the sources and your own knowledge to explain these differences. (6)

(c) Study Sources A, B, C and D.
   Does the evidence of Sources C and D support the view given in Source A or in Source B? Explain your answer. (4)

(d) Study Sources E and F.
   The boom ended very suddenly in October 1929. Use the sources and your own knowledge to explain why this happened. (6)

(e) 'The depression was caused by central government's policy of leaving business alone.'
   Use the sources and your own knowledge to explain whether or not you agree with this statement. (10)

Edexcel Examinations specimen 1998

The United States of America, 1919–41

QUESTIONS

2 (a) What was an 'assembly line'? (4)

   (b) Why was prohibition repealed in 1933? (6)

   (c) The following were features of American society in the 1920s:

      (i) prohibition;

      (ii) motor cars;

      (iii) the cinema.

      Which of these was the most important in changing the lives of American people? Explain your answer, referring to (i), (ii), and (iii). (10)

      MEG specimen papers 1998

3 Study the sources below and then answer the questions which follow.

SOURCE A

An American newspaper cartoon published in 1933.

4 The United States of America, 1919–41

QUESTIONS

SOURCE B

From the new President's first speech, March 1933.

'Let me first of all state that my firm belief is that the only thing we have to fear is fear itself. This nation asks for action, and action now. Our greatest task is to put people to work. This problem can be solved if we face it wisely and courageously. It can be achieved in part by the government itself creating jobs and treating the task as we would treat the emergency of a war.'

SOURCE C

From a historian writing in 1986.

Roosevelt's New Deal caught the imagination of the American people. He offered fresh ideas to help those hard hit by Depression. Above all he gave the American people confidence in themselves and in their President.

SOURCE D

A Republican supporter speaking in 1936.

'Under this government the American people are over-taxed, over-protected and, worst of all, under the control of a single person.'

SOURCE E

Unemployment in the USA, 1930 to 1940.

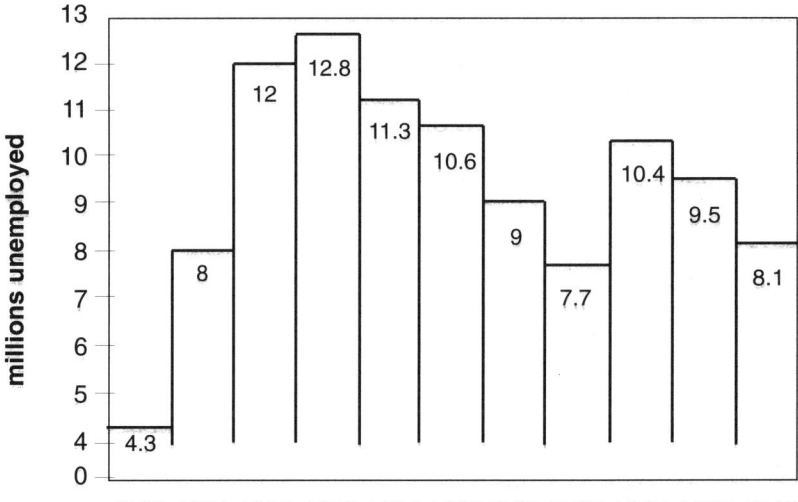

Year	Millions unemployed
1930	4.3
1931	8
1932	12
1933	12.8
1934	11.3
1935	10.6
1936	9
1937	7.7
1938	10.4
1939	9.5
1940	8.1

The United States of America, 1919–41

QUESTIONS

(a) Source A shows one of the President's methods of trying to deal with the Depression. Use your own knowledge to explain the cartoon. (5)

(b) Study Source B.

   (i) What information does Source B give to explain why the New Deal was introduced? (3)

   (ii) Use your own knowledge to say whether the source fully explains why the New Deal was introduced. (3)

(c) Study Sources C and D.

   (i) What different interpretations of the effects of the New Deal are given in Sources C and D? (3)

   (ii) Use your own knowledge to explain why the views presented in the two sources are different. (3)

(d) Study Source E.

'The New Deal achieved its aim: the American people had been "put to work".'
Use your own knowledge to explain whether you agree or disagree with this statement. (8)

(e) What measures did Roosevelt introduce in the 1930s to create employment? How successful were they? (15)

NEAB specimen 1998

5 Events in the 1930s leading to the Second World War

REVISION SUMMARY

1 INTRODUCTION

- Events in the 1930s saw the breakdown of the international security system established by the Treaty of Versailles. This was caused partly by the aggression of Italy, Germany and Japan, and partly by the failure of the League of Nations and the other major powers to stand up to them.

2 ITALY

- In 1922 the leader of the Fascist Party, Mussolini, became Prime Minister of Italy. He was soon dictator. He had dreams of building a great new Italian empire to rival the old Roman empire.
- In 1935 Italy invaded and conquered Ethiopia. The League of Nations did little. In 1936 Mussolini and Hitler set up the Rome-Berlin Axis, agreeing to support each other. Later Japan joined the Axis.

3 GERMANY

- In 1933 Adolf Hitler became Chancellor of Germany. He was helped to power by the economic depression in Germany. He was also popular because he promised to undo many of the provisions of the Treaty of Versailles.
- Hitler wanted to rebuild the German armed forces. He promised to regain land taken from Germany by the Treaty of Versailles, especially those territories where many Germans still lived. He wanted *Anschluss* (union) with Austria and *Lebensraum* (living space) for Germany in the east of Europe.
- Many people in Britain and France believed that the Treaty of Versailles had been unfair to Germany and thought that Hitler's demands were reasonable, especially as he appeared to be a counterbalance to the communist Soviet Union. This led Britain and France into adopting a policy of appeasement towards Hitler. This policy has been criticized by some who claim it convinced Hitler he could get away with his aggressive policies. Others have seen it as a genuine attempt to maintain peace when neither France nor Britain were strong enough to fight. It gave them time to rebuild their armed forces.
- In March 1936 the German army marched into the Rhineland. Neither Britain nor France did anything. Hitler promised that all he wanted now was peace.
- In March 1938 the German army marched into Austria. Austria became part of Germany (*Anschluss*).
- In September 1938 Hitler announced he was prepared to invade the Sudetenland region of Czechoslovakia in order to protect the Germans there. On 29 September, the Munich agreement was reached between Germany, Italy, Britain (represented by Neville Chamberlain) and France. The Sudetenland was given to Germany. Hitler promised that the rest of Czechoslovakia was safe. Chamberlain was sure he had prevented war and returned to Britain in triumph. In March 1939 German troops invaded the rest of Czechoslovakia. Britain and France did nothing.
- In August 1939 Hitler signed the Nazi-Soviet Pact with Stalin. They agreed to divide Poland between them. This left Hitler free to act in the west as he did not have to worry about an attack from the Soviet Union.
- On 1 September 1939 German troops invaded Poland. On 3 September Britain and France declared war on Germany.

4 JAPAN

- Japan was hit hard by the world economic crisis of 1929–33. The country earned all its money by exporting goods, but nobody could afford to buy them. In 1931 Japan invaded Manchuria (part of China). Manchuria had raw materials and would provide a market for Japanese goods. The League of Nations was powerless to act.
- In 1936 Japan signed a pact with Germany. In 1937 Japan invaded the rest of China. In 1941 it invaded Indo-China. The USA replied by banning trade with Japan. In December 1941 the Japanese airforce attacked the American naval base at Pearl Harbor.

If you need to revise this subject more thoroughly, see the relevant topics in the Letts GCSE World History Study Guide.

Events in the 1930s leading to the Second World War

1 Study Source A and then answer all parts of Question 1.

SOURCE A

A photograph taken in March 1939. This photograph shows Czechs giving the Nazi salute as German troops march into Prague, the capital of Czechoslovakia.

(a) Describe the ways in which Germany broke the terms of the Treaty of Versailles in the period 1935–8. (8)

(b) 'The Czech people welcomed the arrival of German troops in Prague.' Does Source A support this view? Explain your answer. (4)

(c) In September 1938 Britain and France were ready to make an agreement with Germany. In September 1939 Britain and France declared war on Germany. Explain why this change came about. (8)

SEG specimen papers 1998

6 The Cold War

REVISION SUMMARY

1 INTRODUCTION

- The 'Cold War' was the period of hostility between the Communist nations (led by the USSR) and the capitalist nations (led by the USA) which followed the Second World War.
- The Cold War never developed into fighting between the USSR and the USA. It was a struggle for influence in the world, created by the hatred which existed between the superpowers.
- The Cold War was at its peak while Stalin was alive. After his death in 1953, the Cold War continued, but as the years passed, tension between the superpowers slowly reduced.

2 THE END OF THE SECOND WORLD WAR

- While the Second World War lasted, the USA and the USSR worked together to defeat the common enemy, the Axis powers. Once the war stopped, hostility between the USSR and the western democracies was bound to surface again.
- As the war came to an end, the Allied leaders met to decide on arrangements for peacemaking, and in particular on the future of Germany and Eastern Europe:
  1. At Yalta (February 1945), they agreed that, once defeated, Germany would be split into four zones of occupation. In Eastern Europe free elections would be held to choose new governments in countries liberated from Germany. The United Nations Organisation would be established as a replacement for the League of Nations.
  2. At Potsdam (July–August 1945), Poland's boundaries were agreed and arrangements for splitting Germany and Berlin into four zones were confirmed.
- However, between the two conferences much had changed. At Yalta, the USA was represented by President Roosevelt, who was prepared to cooperate with Stalin. The Potsdam Conference took place after Roosevelt's death, and his successor, President Truman, was more suspicious of Soviet motives.
- After Yalta, Stalin's determination to force a Communist government on Poland became clearer. Western fears of a Communist takeover in Eastern Europe increased rapidly.
- Soviet suspicion of the USA increased after the atom bomb attacks on Japan. The USA had kept secret the development of this new weapon.
- By 1946, relations between the USSR and the West had deteriorated badly. Churchill, in a speech in the USA, referred to an 'Iron Curtain' which stretched across Europe 'from Stettin in the Baltic to Trieste in the Adriatic'.

3 THE COLD WAR IN EUROPE, 1946–55

- Between 1945 and 1948 most of Eastern Europe fell under the control of Communist governments. These governments were all, with the exception of Yugoslavia which was led by Tito, under Stalin's control.
- Truman was determined to stop the spread of Communism. In 1947, the Truman Doctrine promised that the USA would support any nation threatened by Communist takeover. American and British intervention led to the Communists losing the civil war in Greece.
- In 1947, Truman took another step in fighting Communism by putting forward the Marshall Plan, which promised American aid to European countries to help them rebuild their war-damaged economies.
- The most serious crisis of the early years of the Cold War took place over Berlin in 1948–9. Disagreements over the administration of the zones of occupation, came to a head when the western allies agreed to establish a single government in their zones and to introduce a new currency in order to help Germany's economic recovery. This was completely opposite to Stalin's policy, which was to keep Germany as weak as possible.

The Cold War 6

REVISION SUMMARY

- Berlin, although itself split into four zones, was completely surrounded by the Soviet zone of occupation. In June 1948 Stalin ordered that all land communications between West Berlin and the outside world should be cut off. The Berlin blockade lasted until May 1949 and West Berlin only survived because of the airlift of supplies organised by the western allies. Eventually Stalin gave way. As a result of the crisis, two new states, the German Federal Republic (West Germany) and the German Democratic Republic (East Germany) were set up in 1949.
- In 1949 the western democracies set up a new military alliance called NATO (North Atlantic Treaty Organisation). In 1955 the Soviet Union set up its own alliance, the Warsaw Pact.

4 THE COLD WAR IN ASIA

- The establishment of the Communist regime in China in 1949 caused an extension of the Cold War.
- The outbreak of the Korean War, in 1950, led to the intervention of the USA and other western powers, fighting on behalf of the United Nations, to resist aggression by Communist North Korea against the South. China then joined the war in support of the North. The fighting lasted for three years, at the end of which Korea remained divided.
- Chinese support also helped establish a Communist government in North Vietnam. In 1954 France, the colonial power in Indo-China, was defeated at Dien Bien Phu by the North Vietnamese. The Geneva Agreements of 1954 saw France withdraw from Indo-China. Vietnam was temporarily partitioned, and Laos and Cambodia established as independent states.
- The Geneva Agreements did not solve the problems of Vietnam. By the early 1960s the Americans were giving military help to the South Vietnamese government to prevent a Communist takeover. The fighting in South Vietnam rapidly developed into a full-scale war which continued until 1975 when the Communists took over and reunited the country. The USA had been forced to withdraw from Vietnam by 1973.

5 PEACEFUL COEXISTENCE AND THE CUBAN MISSILE CRISIS

- The process of deStalinisation and the emergence of Khrushchev as the leader of the Soviet Union after 1956 led to a relaxation of tension in the Cold War. The USA did not intervene when the USSR crushed the Hungarian uprising in 1956, and periodic meetings between Soviet and western leaders took place.
- However, in 1960 arrangements for a summit meeting in Paris were thrown into chaos by the shooting down of an American U-2 spy plane over the Soviet Union. The Cold War, for a couple of years, broke out again.
- In 1961, in order to prevent people escaping into West Berlin, the Communist government of East Germany ordered a wall to be built dividing the city into its eastern and western zones. Many people subsequently died trying to cross the wall. The wall became a symbol of Communist tyranny in Eastern Europe.
- In 1962 the most dangerous crisis of the Cold War occurred over Cuba. When the USA discovered that the Soviet Union was constructing missile bases in Cuba, it placed a naval blockade around the island to prevent the bases being completed. The world was threatened with a nuclear war between the superpowers. Eventually Khrushchev backed down and agreed to dismantle the bases.
- The Cuban missile crisis led directly to improved relations between the USA and the USSR. The 'hot line' – a direct telephone line on which the US and Soviet Presidents could talk to each other – was set up, and in 1964 the first major step in limiting nuclear weapons took place with the signing of the Test Ban Treaty.
- Although considerable suspicion between the USA and the USSR remained, relations between the two after 1962 were generally conducted on the basis of peaceful coexistence.

If you need to revise this subject more thoroughly, see the relevant topics in the Letts GCSE World History Study Guide.

6 The Cold War

QUESTIONS

1 (a) This question is about the origins of the Cold War.
Look at the map carefully and then answer questions (i) to (v) which follow.

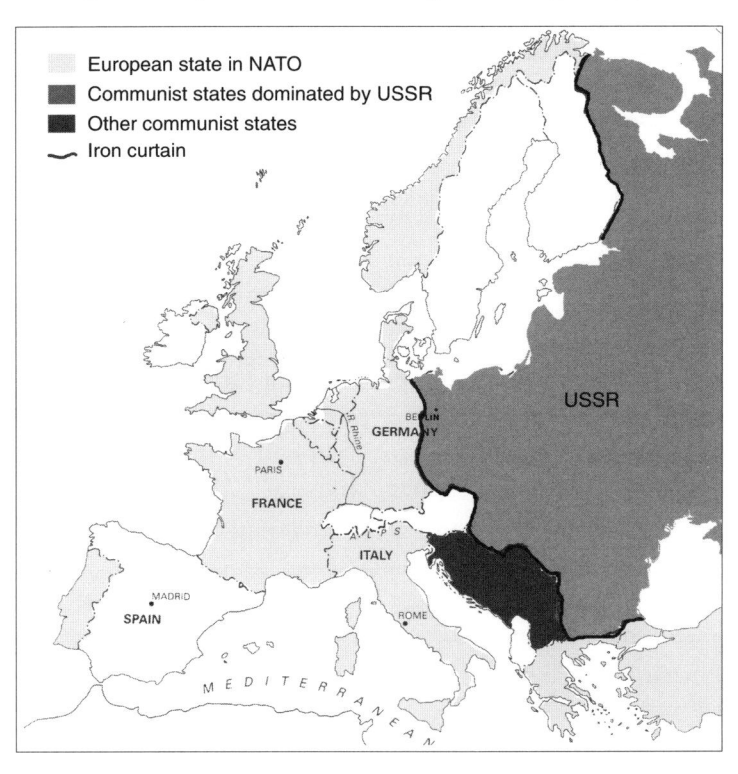

Map legend:
- European state in NATO
- Communist states dominated by USSR
- Other communist states
- Iron curtain

(i) What was meant by the Iron Curtain? (2)

(ii) Give ONE reason why an Iron Curtain appeared in Europe in the years after the Second World War. (3)

(iii) Explain the effects that the Iron Curtain had upon Europe in the years to 1955. (6)

(iv) Why was there a blockade of Berlin from 1948 to 1949? (6)

(v) In what ways did the blockade change relations between the superpowers in the years to 1953? (8)

(b) This question is about the Cuban Missile Crisis.

(i) Why was the US government concerned about events in Cuba from 1960 to 1962? (10)

(ii) Did the Cuban Missile Crisis change relations between the superpowers? Explain your answer. (15)

Edexcel Examinations specimen 1998

2 (a) What were the main aims of the United Nations Organisation when it was set up in 1945? (4)

(b) Explain why the United Nations intervened in Korea in 1950. (6)

(c) How successful was the United Nations' intervention in Korea? Explain your answer. (10)

MEG 1997

The Soviet invasion of Czechoslovakia, 1968

7

REVISION SUMMARY

This section is slightly different from the other sections in this book. This is because it is based on an aspect of the Oxford, Cambridge and RSA [OCR] examination. This syllabus includes as its Paper 2 a source-based investigation of an issue taken from international relations between 1919 and 1989. Each year a different topic is chosen. For the examination in the year 2000 the paper will be on an issue taken from the topic 'Soviet control over Eastern Europe, 1948–68'. Until you see the examination paper itself you will not know exactly what the chosen issue will be, but the following example of a Paper 2 on 'The Soviet invasion of Czechoslovakia, 1968' will give you a good idea of the kinds of questions you will face in the real examination. It is taken from the same topic, it includes the same number of sources and questions, and it tests the same skills. As a sample paper it will provide a very good practice exercise for you. Do not worry if you are not taking the OCR examination. Most of the GCSE Modern World History syllabuses include this topic, and all of them test the skills of using, interpreting and evaluating historical sources which you can practise by doing this exercise.

The OCR Paper 2 will always be set on a topic you have studied. Here are a few guidelines on how to answer the questions on this paper.

❶ Always base your answers on the relevant sources in the paper. Each question will identify certain sources to use. However, be ready, especially in the later questions, to use any other sources if they agree or disagree with the main sources you are using.

❷ You will already have studied and revised the Paper 2 topic for Paper 1. You will not need to know any more about the topic than you have learned for Paper 1. Just because the topic is also coming up on Paper 2 does not mean you need to know anything extra about it.

❸ You should use your knowledge of the topic in a number of ways.
(i) Use your knowledge to help you to understand what a source is saying.
(ii) Use your knowledge to evaluate sources for reliability. For example, you might know from your knowledge of a topic that what a source is claiming is either right or wrong, or you might have some knowledge about the author or artist of a source which allows you to judge how reliable a source is likely to be.

❹ When you are evaluating a source try and consider the following: what the source says, who wrote or drew the source, what his or her purpose might be, and what your knowledge of the topic tells you about what the source is saying.

❺ In your answers, do not use only the sources and ignore your knowledge of the topic; and do not use only your knowledge and ignore the sources. Use both – all the time.

❻ When you are trying to understand what a source is saying, try and go beyond the surface features of the source. This is especially important with cartoons where the artist will be using what he or she has drawn, as symbols to represent something else.

❼ When you are evaluating sources, do not fall into the trap of deciding whether or not a source is reliable simply by its type. For example, all primary sources are reliable, newspaper accounts cannot be trusted, eye-witness accounts can be trusted, photographs are always posed and so on. All of these statements are wrong because they are too sweeping. We cannot generalise about sources in this way. Some primary sources will be reliable, others will not. The same can be said of all types of sources. You need to judge each source on its own merits and think about what it says, who wrote or drew it, and why they wrote or drew it.

❽ When you are using a source to support your answer, do make sure that you say which source it is and do support your answer by referring to specific details in the source.

❾ Do not spend too long on the early questions. Generally speaking, the questions at the end of the paper will carry more marks and you must make sure you answer these properly.

❿ The final one or two questions on the paper will often ask you to reach some kind of conclusion about the topic using all the sources together. Do not write a separate paragraph on each source. Try and form a conclusion in your mind, or on rough paper, and then build a case, using the sources and your knowledge, supporting it.

If you need to revise this subject more thoroughly, see the relevant topics in the Letts GCSE World History Study Guide.

7 The Soviet invasion of Czechoslovakia, 1968

QUESTIONS

DID THE SOVIET UNION HAVE TO INVADE CZECHOSLOVAKIA IN 1968?

Read the introduction and the sources, and then answer the questions which follow.

INTRODUCTION

In December 1967 Alexander Dubček became leader of the Communist state of Czechoslovakia. He was a reformer who wanted to relax the tight control of the Communist Party over the economy and society. He allowed the Czechoslovakian people more freedom. His policy of 'Socialism with a Human Face' worried the leaders of the Soviet Union. They feared that Dubček's ideas could cause trouble in other Communist countries, and possibly even lead to the collapse of Communist power in Eastern Europe. In August 1968 troops from the Soviet Union and other Warsaw Pact countries invaded Czechoslovakia. Dubček was overthrown, and a new leader, more loyal to Moscow, was appointed. The experiments of the 'Prague Spring' were over.

But why did the Soviet Union think it necessary to invade? Was the 'Prague Spring' really a threat to Communist power?

SOURCE A

> **From a speech given in Czechoslovakia in March 1968.**
>
> The people who were trusted by the Communist government were the obedient ones, those who did not cause any trouble, who did not ask any questions. It was the mediocre man who came off best. In twenty years not one human problem has been solved in our country; from basic needs like flats, to the need for people to trust one another, to the need for education. I feel that our country has lost its good reputation.

SOURCE B

> **From a letter of warning sent by the Soviet Union to the Czech leaders in July 1968.**
>
> Developments in your country are causing deep anxiety among us. We are convinced that your country is being pushed off the road to socialism and that this puts in danger the whole socialist system. We cannot accept the risk of Czechoslovakia being cut off from the socialist community of countries. This is something more than your own concern, it is the common concern of all communist parties and states.

SOURCE C

> **A statement by the Soviet government on 21 August 1968, the morning after the invasion of Czechoslovakia.**
>
> Leaders of the Czechoslovak Socialist Republic have asked the Soviet Union and other allied states to render the Czechoslovak people urgent assistance, including assistance with armed forces. This request was brought about by the threat which had arisen to the socialist system in Czechoslovakia. Nobody will ever be allowed to pull apart a single link from the community of socialist states.

The Soviet invasion of Czechoslovakia, 1968

SOURCE D

From a radio broadcast by the Czechoslovak Communist Party, 21 August 1968.

Yesterday around 11.00 pm troops of the Soviet Union, Poland, East Germany, Hungary and Bulgaria crossed our frontiers. This happened without the knowledge of the President of the Republic, the Prime Minister or the First Secretary of the central committee of the Communist Party. The central committee appeals to all citizens of our republic to maintain calm and not offer resistance to the troops on the march. Our army, security corps and people's militia have not received the command to defend the country.

The central committee regards this invasion as against not only the fundamental principles of relations between socialist states but also as against the principles of international law.

SOURCE E

A Czechoslovakian street cartoon, 1968.

SOURCE F

A Czechoslovakian street cartoon, 1968. It shows Lenin weeping.

7 The Soviet invasion of Czechoslovakia, 1968

QUESTIONS

SOURCE G

A Czech protester in Prague argues with a Soviet soldier, August 1968.

The Soviet invasion of Czechoslovakia, 1968

SOURCE H

An American cartoon about the Soviet invasion of Czechoslovakia, 1968. It shows Dubček in between the two Soviet leaders.

SOURCE I

An extract from a recent textbook on Modern World History.

The Russian leader, Brezhnev, defended his actions. He said that a threat to communist rule in any country in Eastern Europe gave other communist countries the right to step in to crush the threat. This 'Brezhnev Doctrine' was a clear warning to other countries in Eastern Europe. This is our patch, the Russians were saying. We will have the final say about any changes that are made here.

7 The Soviet invasion of Czechoslovakia, 1968

QUESTIONS Now answer **all** the following questions.

1. Read Source A.
   What can you tell about the situation in Czechoslovakia in early 1968 from this source? (6)

2. Read Source B.
   How far does this source explain why the Soviet Union invaded Czechoslovakia in 1968? Explain your answer. (8)

3. Read Sources C and D.
   Does Source D prove the Soviet government is lying in Source C?
   Explain your answer. (9)

4. Study Sources E and G.
   How similar are these two sources?
   Explain your answer. (9)

5. Study Source F.
   Does this source show that the Czechs supported Communism or not?
   Explain your answer. (8)

6. Study Source H.
   What was the cartoonist's opinion of Soviet actions towards Czechoslovakia?
   Explain your answer using details of the cartoon. (8)

7. Use **all** the sources.
   How far do these sources show that it was not really necessary for the Soviet Union to invade Czechoslovakia in 1968?
   Explain your answer. (12)

Mock examination paper 8

WHY DID THE USA INTRODUCE THE MARSHALL PLAN?

QUESTIONS

Background Information

In June 1947 General George Marshall, a member of the US government, offered financial support to European countries to help them recover from the devastation caused by the Second World War. The leaders of 16 west European countries met and agreed a recovery plan which became known as the Marshall Plan.

Over the next four years $13,000 million of help was provided. Stalin did not allow any Eastern European countries to apply for the aid because he saw the Marshall Plan as an attempt by the USA to control Europe. The USA, on the other hand, claimed it was to stop the USSR and Communism taking over Europe.

SOURCE A

An extract from a British history book published in 1984.

> President Truman felt that Communism did well when people were poor and suffering and that it could be resisted by economic aid and prosperity. In 1947, a member of his government, General Marshall, put forward a plan to give billions of dollars of aid to Europe. He saw that most of western Europe was still shattered from the war and would need help to recover. If Western Europe did not recover, the USA would be left on its own to face the Russians. Western European countries had to be made strong enough to defend themselves. The US Congress was not keen on the idea but, just as they were discussing it, came the news of the brutal Communist take-over of Czechoslovakia. Congress then voted to give 4 million dollars.
>
> There are differing views about Marshall Aid. It could appear to be generous help to a weak Europe. It could appear that it was given to build up strong anti-Communist countries. Another view is that it was designed to help American industry by creating markets for American goods.

Mock examination paper

QUESTIONS

SOURCE B

A cartoon about Marshall Aid, published in the USSR in 1948.

Do not sow seed. I will sell you maize.

Do not build new shipyards. I will sell you old ones cheaply.

why do you want to strengthen your currency? Why don't you try mine?

It is difficult to carry out your policy? Carry out ours!

SOURCE C

A cartoon about Marshall Aid, published in the USA in 1949.

I LOVE THE GUY, BUT SOMETIMES I THINK HE'S TOO GOOD!

U.S. TAXPAYER

TO ALL PARTS OF THE WORLD

Mock examination paper 8

QUESTIONS

SOURCE D

The USSR's spokesman at the United Nations, speaking in September 1947.

> As is now clear, the Marshall Plan is clearly just another version of the Truman Doctrine adapted to the conditions of post-war Europe. It will place European countries under the economic and political control of the United States. In bringing forward this plan, the United States government counted on the co-operation of the governments of Britain and France to limit freedom of choice in Europe.

SOURCE E

The USSR's spokesman at the Cominform Conference in September 1947. (Cominform was the Communist Information Bureau designed to coordinate the activities of the Communist Party throughout Europe.)

> The Truman Doctrine and the Marshall Plan are both part of an American plan to enslave Europe. The United States has launched an attack on the principle of each nation being in charge of its own affairs. By contrast, the Soviet Union is defending the principle of real equality and independence among nations. The Soviet Union will make every effort to ensure that the Marshall Plan is doomed to failure.

SOURCE F

From a speech by an American politician in 1948.

> The Marshall Plan is designed to stop the friendly and democratic parts of Europe from collapsing. The iron curtain must not come to the edge of the Atlantic.

8 Mock examination paper

QUESTIONS Study the Background Information and the sources carefully, and then answer all the questions which follow.

In answering the questions you are expected to use your knowledge of the topic to help you interpret and evaluate the sources and to explain your answers. When you are instructed to use a source you must do so, but you may also use any of the other sources which are relevant.

1 Study Source A.

   According to Source A, why did the USA introduce the Marshall Plan? (5)

2 Study Source B.

   Do you think the cartoonist approved of the Marshall Plan? Explain your answer referring to details of the cartoon and your own knowledge. (5)

3 Study Sources B and C.

   How far does Source C agree with Source B about the Marshall Plan? Explain your answer by referring to details of the two cartoons and your own knowledge. (6)

4 Study Sources D and E.

   Sources D and E agree about the Marshall Plan. Does this mean that they are reliable? Use your own knowledge to help you explain your answer. (6)

5 Study Source F and all the other sources.

   How far do the other sources support the claim made in Source F that the Marshall Plan was introduced to protect democratic countries from Communism? Explain your answer. Make sure you use your own knowledge to interpret and evaluate the sources. (8)

Answers

1 THE PEACE TREATIES OF 1919-20 AND THE LEAGUE OF NATIONS

Answer	Mark

1 **(a) Look at Source A. What is the cartoonist saying about the League of Nations? Explain your answer, referring to details in the cartoon.** (5)

Examiner's tip — This question requires you to interpret Source A, which shows Uncle Sam (the USA) leaning against the keystone which is missing from the bridge. The bridge represents the League of Nations. Uncle Sam is looking as if he is in no hurry to have anything to do with the League, and, as we know, the USA refused to become a member. The fact that the bridge is not complete is bound to make it weaker.
In your answer you must use details of the cartoon to back up your interpretation of what the cartoonist was trying to say about the League. Don't just describe what the cartoon shows; your task is to explain what the cartoon means. The following example does this well.

The cartoonist thought the League of Nations would not be a success because it would be too weak. He shows the League as a bridge which is not completed. The bit that is missing is the most important – the keystone which holds the bridge together. Without the keystone the bridge can never be strong. The USA was the bit missing from the League of Nations, because they refused to join. This is why Uncle Sam is shown lying on the ground, not attempting to complete the bridge. The cartoonist is saying that the USA was the most important country of all, and without it the League cannot be strong.

(b) What did the Great Powers want to achieve when they set up the League of Nations? (5)

Examiner's tip — This question is not asking you to explain an event; it is simply asking you to recall information about the aims of the Great Powers in creating the League of Nations. The number of marks available should be a useful guide to you in judging how much to write. Clearly, a simple answer like 'They wanted to keep the peace' is not going to be enough on its own. On the other hand, a lengthy answer is obviously not required. With questions like these, giving two or three aims with some detail on each will be enough to gain full marks.

The most important reason the Great Powers had for setting up the League was they wanted to avoid any more wars. They believed that all future disputes could be settled without using force. They would achieve this in various ways. Members had to agree to use arbitration. If one nation threatened to use force all the other nations would join against them. Sanctions could be used against an aggressor. Another reason they had for creating the League was to try and settle some of the world's problems by co-operating with each other. The League had many agencies which dealt with issues like refugees, women's rights, drugs and workers' rights. Finally, they also used the League to deal with the mandates created by the peace treaties. The countries given the mandates were answerable to the League.

2 **(a) What limits did the Treaty of Versailles place on Germany's military strength?** (4)

Examiner's tip — This is another question which requires only recall from you. The Treaty of Versailles limited Germany's military strength in several different ways. You are not expected to remember them all to gain full marks. Given that four marks are available, it is a fair bet that listing four different restrictions will be enough, but be careful – the question asks only for military terms of the Treaty, and nothing else will do.

Answers to Unit 1

Answer	Mark

The Treaty tried to destroy Germany's military strength. It was not allowed to have an air force. Its army was limited to 100 000 men. It was not allowed to have any submarines. Finally, the Rhineland was demilitarised, which meant that Germany could not put any troops there.

(b) Why did the victorious powers want to limit Germany's strength? (6)

> **Examiner's tip** You will come across many questions like this one, which ask 'Why?' something happened. Never fall into the trap of giving just one cause – all events have many causes, and some causes are more important than others. In this particular question, however, only six marks are at stake, so the explanation you are expected to provide cannot be all that lengthy or detailed. Concentrate on what you think were the most important causes, and show how they worked together to bring the event about.

There are lots of reasons why they wanted to limit Germany's strength after the First World War. Other nations feared Germany because they knew that militarily and economically she was the strongest nation in Europe. They did not want another war, they were all exhausted by the war which had just finished. They blamed Germany for the war, and wanted to punish her. So it's not that surprising that they produced a harsh treaty for Germany to sign. If you take something like the demilitarisation of the Rhineland, you can see that it was a punishment and a humiliation, but it was also intended to make Germany weak and unable to protect herself, thus making another war unlikely. This explains why the Allies were so determined to limit Germany's strength.

(c) 'The most important reason why Germany hated the Treaty of Versailles was the military restrictions.' Do you agree with this statement? Explain your answer. (10)

> **Examiner's tip** This question is concerned with the reasons why the Germans hated the Treaty of Versailles. The question mentions the military restrictions but there were other reasons why the Germans hated the Treaty, and your answer needs to consider these too. Then you need to reach a judgement on which reason for hating the Treaty was the most important, but be aware that this also involves showing why other reasons were less important. You might conclude that they were all important, and contributed together in making the Germans hate the Treaty. This need not stop you saying that one reason was more important than the others.

The Germans certainly resented the military restrictions of the Treaty. These restrictions, such as limiting the army to 100 000 men, left Germany almost defenceless, which for a great power was a humiliation. However, there were other aspects of the Treaty which caused even more controversy. First, it was a 'Diktat', the Germans were forced to accept it. They thought it was unfair, particularly as the Kaiser had abdicated at the end of the war, and the new democratic government in Germany expected to be treated fairly. Second, the Allies blamed Germany for the war through the 'War Guilt Clause', and this enabled them to claim damages (reparations) from Germany. Most Germans did not accept that they were the only ones to blame. Third, Germany lost much of its territory and all its colonies, which together with the reparations did a lot to undermine the German economy, creating poverty and unemployment. All of these aspects of the Treaty were hated, not just the military restrictions.

Of all these reasons for hating the Treaty, I think the War Guilt Clause was the most important. The reason for this is that it gave the Allies the excuse to do all the other

Answers to Unit 2

Answer	Mark

things in the Treaty. If Germany was to blame, she deserved to be punished. So all of the other points in the Treaty were consequences of this one, and are therefore less important in themselves. Of course, you cannot just take one aspect of the Treaty and say it explains on its own why the Germans hated the Treaty. If the Allies had not taken away any land, or had not insisted on reparations, then the Germans would not have hated the Treaty so much. So all the reasons were important, but one was more important than the others.

2 GERMANY, 1919–39

Answer	Mark

1 **(a) During 1923 the Weimar Republic was threatened by these events:
(i) the French invasion of the Ruhr; (ii) the inflation of the mark;
(iii) the Beer-Hall Putsch.
Describe any one of these events.** (4)

Examiner's tip The allocation of four marks to this question tells you that a relatively brief answer will be sufficient. The command word 'Describe' in the question indicates that you are not expected to do anything more than say what happened – no analysis or explanation is needed. You should aim to write a summary of the events in a single paragraph. Make at least four clear points; in questions requiring description alone it is a reasonable assumption that each valid point will earn a mark. The examples given below show you how to earn full marks on each of the three events. You should do as the question tells you and answer on only one.

(i) By early 1923 the French were fed up with Germany not paying reparations, so in January French and Belgian troops marched into the Ruhr and occupied it (1). This was a considerable blow to Germany as the Ruhr was one of her most important industrial areas (1). The French intended to take their reparations in coal instead of money, but the German workers refused to co-operate and went on strike (1). The occupation was only brought to an end when the German government promised in September to resume reparations payments (1).

(ii) The German mark was already losing its value quickly even before 1923, because the Germans could not afford to pay reparations and so were just printing more money to try and cover their debts (1). During 1923 this inflation got much worse, mainly because of the French occupation of the Ruhr (1). In this period of hyper-inflation the mark became more or less worthless, with billions of marks being needed to buy a loaf of bread (1). People who had savings lost all their money, but people who owed money were happy because the debts simply disappeared (1).

(iii) The Nazis in Bavaria took advantage of all the disasters of 1923 to try and seize power; this became known as the Beer-Hall Putsch (1). Hitler and his supporters interrupted a political meeting in a Munich beer hall, and forced some of Bavaria's political leaders to declare their support for a Nazi takeover (1). The next day a column of Nazis marched into the centre of Munich but they met resistance from the army and police, and the Putsch collapsed (1). Hitler was later arrested, put on trial, and imprisoned for his part in the Putsch (1).

Answers to Unit 2

Answer	Mark

(b) Why was the Weimar Republic able to survive the events of 1923? (6)

> **Examiner's tip** As with all other 'Why?' questions you must consider a range of causes, but in this particular question you also need to decide what the phrase 'the events of 1923' covers. Look again at question (a) – this gives you three events of 1923 which threatened the Weimar Republic. The best answers will cover each of these three events. Another point to bear in mind is that your answer should not just give reasons why the Republic was able to survive; it should also explain why these reasons were important. The following answer is just a list of reasons:

The Weimar Republic was able to survive the events of 1923 because Stresemann called off the strikes in the Ruhr, negotiated a loan from the Americans, and the Beer-Hall Putsch collapsed.

> **Examiner's tip** All this is true, but it does not provide a proper explanation. The next example shows why each of the reasons was significant. This is obviously a much stronger answer, and would earn full marks.

In August 1923 Stresemann became Chancellor of Germany. He realised that solutions had to be found quickly to Germany's problems. He called off the strikes in the Ruhr and promised to pay Germany's reparations. The mines and factories started working again, and the French agreed to withdraw their troops. He took steps to stabilise the currency, withdrawing all the useless money, and setting up a new currency, the Rentenmark. In 1924 the Dawes Plan, negotiated with the USA, made substantial loans to Germany, which enabled the economy to recover further. These measures brought economic life in Germany back to a normal condition. Meanwhile, the collapse of the Beer-Hall Putsch and the imprisonment of leading Nazis had shown that the Republic was capable of dealing firmly with political extremists. The army and the police had stayed loyal to the Republic, and had not sided with the Nazis.

(c) Did the events of 1923 make the Weimar Republic weaker or stronger? Explain your answer. (10)

> **Examiner's tip** This question is asking you to analyse the consequences of the events of 1923. There is no correct answer; you may decide either that the Republic was weakened or strengthened. However, good answers will show awareness of the fact that in some ways the Republic was weakened, but in other ways it was strengthened.

> **Examiner's tip** This paragraph identifies ways in which the Republic was weakened by the events of 1923.

The Republic survived the events of 1923, but it was significantly weakened by them. The occupation of German territory by the French was a national humiliation, and gave enemies of the Republic within Germany plenty of encouragement. The hyper-inflation wiped out the savings of the middle classes and turned many of them permanently against the Republic. It is no accident that the Nazis attracted more support from

Answers to Unit 2

Answer   **Mark**

amongst the lower-middle classes than from any other group. Even the crushing of the Beer-Hall Putsch turned into a curious triumph for Hitler, who was able to use his trial as propaganda for Nazi ideas, and turn the Nazis into a nationally recognised party.

> **Examiner's tip** This paragraph identifies ways in which the Republic was strengthened by the events of 1923.

Of course, you cannot deny that after 1923 things got better for the Republic. The French withdrew from the Ruhr, and the economy recovered rapidly, helped by US loans in the Dawes Plan and the rescheduling of reparations payments. Political extremists had been dealt with, and played little part in the politics of Germany for the next five years. Hitler was in jail, and his party was banned. Although Stresemann was Chancellor for only a few months, he remained Foreign Minister until 1929, and had many foreign policy successes.

> **Examiner's tip** This paragraph reaches a conclusion which shows how a judgement on whether the Republic was made stronger or weaker depends on the timescale on which the answer is based.

I think the Republic was made stronger in the short term, but weaker in the long term, by what happened in 1923. It survived in 1923, so in that sense you could say it got stronger because it recovered, and indeed the years 1924-9 were years of achievement and stability for the Republic. But when the next crisis came along it would be less able to cope, because people would remember how it had failed them before. All the enemies the Republic made in 1923 – the middle classes who had lost their savings, the Nationalists humiliated by the occupation of the Ruhr and Germany's dependence on American loans – would not defend the Republic when it got into difficulties in 1929. This is one of the reasons why the Republic was eventually unable to survive the crisis of 1929-33.

---

2 (a) Source A gives four extracts from the Nazi Party Programme of 1920. Use your own knowledge to explain why these were likely to win support for the Nazi Party. (5)

> **Examiner's tip** The task here is to look at the four points and explain why each of them would be likely to appeal to Germans in 1920. The allocation of five marks indicates that you do not have to write much on each point. The following example takes each point in turn and gives specific reasons why it would attract the support of some or all Germans. It would easily score full marks.

Point 1 would attract support because many Germans, such as those in the Sudetenland, lived outside Germany. The peacemakers had promised self-determination to all people – why should this not apply to Germans too?

Point 2 would have been supported by all Germans. The Treaty was the hated 'Diktat', which humiliated Germany in many different ways – limiting her armed forces, taking territory away, making her pay reparations, and so on.

Point 3 was Hitler's idea of 'lebensraum'. This would not be so important to many Germans, but much of Germany's eastern lands had been lost in the Treaty of Versailles, and they would want these back.

Answers to Unit 2

Answer	Mark

Point 4 would appeal particularly to those who hated the Jews. The Nazis appealed to German anti-semitism, and blamed the Jews, amongst others, for Germany's defeat in the war. This was called the 'Stab in the Back'.

(b) (i) Study Source B. What evidence is there in the source to suggest that it might not be reliable to an historian writing about why Hitler won support before 1933? (3)

> **Examiner's tip** Questions on the reliability of sources are used a lot in GCSE History papers. You are being asked whether or not you can believe what the source says. Weak answers will fall into the trap of assuming that you cannot believe what Speer wrote because he was a Nazi, or because he was writing after the Second World War. The problem with these answers is that they ignore the content of the source. Never limit your answer in this way. The content of the source is the most important single factor in helping you decide whether or not the source is reliable. Read the source, and then ask yourself a simple question: 'In the light of what I know about this topic, do I believe what the source tells me?' If the source agrees with what you know to be the facts, then it does not matter whether it was written by a Nazi, or was written after the Second World War. Even Nazis sometimes told the truth. With this question, however, the issue is slightly more complex. Here we have to judge how reliable the source is as evidence on why the Nazis gained support before 1933. Source B could be the truth as Speer saw it, but still not be reliable evidence for our purpose. With only three marks at stake, a lengthy analysis is obviously not required, but a good answer should indicate awareness of these issues. The following example does this well.

Source B is a Nazi view of why Hitler attracted support before 1933. The things that attracted Speer might not have been what attracted other people, so we would have to be careful about accepting it as completely reliable evidence.

It's reliable as a Nazi view, and certainly fear of Communism and unemployment, and the desire for order, won the Nazis support, but other people might have mentioned other reasons for voting for the Nazis, like disillusionment with the Weimar Republic which could not solve Germany's problems.

(b) (ii) Study Source B. Use your own knowledge to explain what parts of Source B can be accepted as accurate by an historian writing about why Hitler won support before 1933. (3)

> **Examiner's tip** Even though Source B is the viewpoint of a Nazi, it contains references which are factual. This question asks you to identify those aspects of the source that are fact rather than opinion. Identification and explanation of three references in the source would certainly be enough to gain full marks.

Source B is based on fact. In 1931 there was 'hopeless unemployment' – over four million were unemployed, the number was still increasing and the government seemed unable to do anything to stop it. The Nazis did have parades, and used them deliberately to give an impression of strength and order – it was part of their propaganda technique. You could even say that the Nazis gave people hope – Hitler promised to make Germany great again and to solve the unemployment crisis.

(c) (i) Study Source C. Why might Source C be useful as evidence to explain why the Nazis became the largest party in the Reichstag in 1933? (3)

Answers to Unit 2

Answer	Mark

> **Examiner's tip** This question is looking for an interpretation of the source in the context of events in Germany in 1932–3. The poster shows a message that the Nazi Party was trying to get across to the German people. It shows a crowd of hopeless, dispirited people, for whom Hitler is the last hope. Obviously it refers to the millions of unemployed people in Germany at that time, and suggests that only the Nazis can help them. If this is a message that many German people accepted, then obviously it helps to explain why the Nazis won the largest number of seats in the Reichstag elections of 1932–3. The following answer shows how to gain all three marks by linking the message of the source to the Nazis' victory in 1933.

This poster comes from 1932 but its message was just as relevant in 1933. The Nazis said they could solve Germany's unemployment problem. The poster says they were Germany's last hope for all the millions of unemployed. Enough people believed them to win the largest number of seats in the 1933 election

(c) (ii) Study Source C. Use your own knowledge to say whether the source fully explains why the Nazis became the largest party in the Reichstag in 1932. (3)

> **Examiner's tip** Whenever a question asks you whether something 'fully explains' something else, your first reaction should be 'No, of course not, there must be other reasons.' Certainly Source C helps to explain why the Nazis became the largest party in the Reichstag in 1932, and your answer can mention this, but you need to identify other reasons too. As there are only three marks for this question, mentioning a couple of other reasons would probably be sufficient to earn full marks, as in the following example.

Source C does cover some of the reasons why Hitler won the 1932 elections. Fear of unemployment, and hope that the Nazis could do something about it, certainly helped Hitler to win. But there were other reasons not shown in Source C. Hitler's own personality and appeal as a leader was a major factor. So was the organisation and discipline of the Nazis. Perhaps the single biggest reason for their victory was that people believed that the Weimar Republic had failed and was powerless to solve Germany's problems. So Source C cannot fully explain all the reasons.

(d) Study Source D. 'The events of February and March 1933 allowed Hitler and the Nazis to take full control of Germany by August 1934.' Use your own knowledge to explain whether you agree or disagree with this statement. (8)

> **Examiner's tip** In this question the source is provided to give you information. You are not expected to treat it as evidence. It simply tells you what the most important events of February and March 1933 were. In a way, this question is similar to question (c)(ii) above.
> You are asked whether it was the events of February and March 1933 which gave Hitler full control of Germany. Again, your response should be that they helped, but that there were other reasons which also contributed; in other words, it was not the events of February and March 1933 alone which gave Hitler full control. A full explanation, like the following one, must deal both with events in February and March 1933, and with later events, showing how each helped Hitler to achieve full power by August 1934.

Answers to Unit 2

Answer	Mark

The events of February and March 1933 were important in Hitler's rise to power because they resulted in Hitler becoming Dictator over Germany. The Reichstag Fire came in the middle of the campaign for the March 1933 election. Hitler used it to launch an anti-Communist scare, banning the Communist Party and arresting many of its leaders. Despite this terror campaign, Hitler still did not win an outright majority in the election, but with his allies, the Nationalists, and by intimidating other parties, he was able to force the Reichstag to pass the Enabling Law. This gave him the power to make any laws he wanted, and he used it to ban other parties, outlaw trade unions, and suppress free speech. However, he did not yet have total power.

Hindenburg was still President of Germany. Although old and weak he prevented Hitler achieving total power. The army, for instance, regarded themselves as loyal to the President and not to the Chancellor. Even within the Nazi Party Hitler faced problems. It was not until 1934 that these could be dealt with. Once the Nazis came to power, the SA expected Hitler to give them special treatment and favours. Their leader, Rohm, wanted the SA to be turned into a revolutionary people's army, a development the real army viewed with horror. Hitler could not afford to lose the army's goodwill; instead he turned on the SA. In 'the Night of the Long Knives' (in June 1934) Hitler had all his enemies, including Rohm, murdered. The threat of the SA had been crushed. In August, Hindenburg died. Hitler took over the office of President, and had the army swear an oath of loyalty to him as 'Führer' (leader) of the German people. This was the point at which he achieved full power.

In conclusion, you can say that the events of February and March 1933 were very important in giving Hitler power in Germany, but that events after these months gave him total power, because it was not until August 1934 that he could be sure that all significant opposition had been dealt with.

EITHER

(e) (i) Why was Germany hit by depression in 1929? Why was the Weimar Republic unable to deal with it? (15)

> **Examiner's tip** Here you face two 'Why?' questions in one. You must answer each in turn, remembering the advice you have been given on earlier questions of this type – all events have multiple causes. You should identify these, and explain how they worked together to bring about the events in question. The large number of marks allocated to this question is an indication that it is worth writing in as much detail as you can within the time available. The following answer gives you an idea of the length and level of detail you should aim for.

The Wall Street Crash in the USA in October 1929 was the single most important cause of the depression which hit Germany. The Crash led in time to a collapse of world trade which hit all countries badly. However, Germany was hit worse than most because of its dependence on American loans. These came to a halt, which exposed all the fundamental weaknesses of the German economy. Even before the Crash German agriculture had been in depression; now production in German industry fell alarmingly, creating mass unemployment, which in turn depressed demand for manufactured goods still more. In other words, the Wall Street Crash sparked off a chain reaction which plunged Germany into depression.

The Weimar government was ill-equipped to deal with the depression. Like all other western governments, its first reaction was to try and deal with the crisis by cutting government expenditure. This was the worst possible course to take, but at the time they thought

Answers to Unit 2

Answer	Mark

that spending government money to create jobs would produce a return to the years of hyper-inflation. You could say that the memory of earlier troubles now made it harder for the Republic to cope. Politically, it was in deep trouble. None of the democratic parties had any idea of how to deal with the crisis, leaving government in the hands of Hindenburg and a succession of weak Chancellors. Extremists like the Nazis and the Communists were doing all they could to bring the Republic down. Meanwhile, unemployment rose to over 5 million. Looking back on that time we can see that spending its way out of the Depression, as Hitler proposed, and as Roosevelt did in America, was probably the best course to take, but this was not at all obvious at the time. The political problems of the Republic made it impossible for the economic problems to be solved, and they were only eventually solved by Hitler's rearmament programme, hardly an option open to a democratic government.

OR

(ii) What measures did Hitler take between 1934 and 1939 to bring employment to the German people? How successful was he? (15)

> **Examiner's tip** Again, the number of marks indicates that you are expected to write a detailed and extended answer. You are asked first to describe Hitler's employment policies, and then to judge their success. You could do this as two separate sections in your answer, or you could weave the description and the analysis together. The following example takes the first approach. The advantage of doing this is that the Examiner cannot be in any doubt about what each section of your answer is trying to achieve.

Hitler promised to solve the unemployment problem in Germany and he took many steps to achieve this. The most significant was the rearmament programme. Many men went into the armed forces, others went into the armaments industries. Huge amounts of government money went into this programme. This in turn created employment in other industries supplying raw materials like coal and iron. There was also a huge programme of public works. The unemployed were recruited to do this work. The most famous result was the autobahns, but many impressive public buildings were also constructed. Employers were encouraged to take on more workers than they needed and not to sack workers that they already employed. In return, Hitler banned trade unions and made sure pay did not rise too much. Women were encouraged to stay at home and have children, rather than going out to work.

It cannot be disputed that Hitler solved the problem of unemployment. By 1939 it had almost disappeared. The problem is the price that Germany and Europe had to pay. German unemployment disappeared because Germany was preparing for war. The German economy could not support the cost of this programme for ever. The German people had to give up their freedom in order to get jobs. Many of the jobs on public works schemes were little better than slave labour. There was much hidden unemployment, as employers were pressured not to sack workers. However, most German people did have a rising standard of living up to 1939, more consumer goods were produced as well as armaments.

3 By 1939 the Nazis had been in power in Germany for six years. Were German working people better off in 1939 than they had been in 1933? Explain your answer. (12)

Answers to Unit 2

Answer	Mark

> **Examiner's tip** The number of marks available is an indication that you are expected to write an answer of some length. You should aim to write a couple of paragraphs at least, but more important than the *amount* you write is the *quality* of your answer. Just because the question invites an extended response, you must not simply write all you know about the topic. *Plan* your answer. Try to think of arguments on both sides of the question. Were the Germans better off by 1939 in some ways, but worse off in other ways? Here an obvious plan would be: paragraph one, how the Germans were better off; paragraph two, how they were worse off; paragraph three, conclusion. The answer below follows this plan, and would be worth full marks.

One of Hitler's greatest achievements was ending unemployment in Germany. Of course, he only did this by planning for war, but rearmament and military service meant that almost everyone had a job. Given that around 5 million were unemployed when Hitler came to power, you could say that most Germans were better off in 1939. The real value of wages rose up to 1939 and Nazi labour organisations improved working conditions and arranged all kinds of sporting and social activities. So although industrial workers were expected to work longer hours, most of them felt that they were better off because of the Nazis. In the country as a whole there was a feeling that the Nazis had made Germany great again, and most Germans shared a sense of pride at what had been achieved.

However, there were some ways in which life was not better. Germany under the Nazis was a police state. People were not free. If you opposed the Nazis, you could be imprisoned, and many opponents were murdered. Workers lost all their rights. They could not strike for more pay. They had to do what they were told and accept what they were given. All aspects of life were controlled. Germans had to put up with endless Nazi propaganda. There was compulsory military service, and it was obvious that war was a strong possibility.

The Nazis were helped into power by the unemployment created by the Depression. Most people were grateful to them for solving the unemployment problem, and were prepared to put up with a loss of freedom as the price they had to pay. They turned a blind eye to the prison camps, and to the persecution of groups like the Jews. You can understand why they felt like this at the time, but looking back we can see the evil of the Nazis was bound to bring disaster for Germany. German people in 1939 might have felt better off, but the reality was that they were being ruled by criminals.

3 RUSSIA, 1917–41

Answer	Mark

1 (a) Study Source A. What can you learn from Source A about the situation in Petrograd in March 1917? (4)

Answers to Unit 3

Answer	Mark

Examiner's tip Answering this question you need to consider both what the source tells us and who wrote the source and what this might tell us. The source tells us that there was unrest in Petrograd. The fact that it is written by the Tsarina and she is dismissive towards the unrest tells us that she did not take the unrest seriously. The answer which follows covers both of these points and would be awarded high marks.

The source tells me that there was unrest. People are protesting because food prices were high and they were starving. There was food but it was not getting to the towns because the railway system fell into chaos. The Tsarina, who was in control of the government while the Tsar commanded the army, did not care about this. She thinks the protesters are hooligans and that the protests will fade away, especially if it gets cold. This shows she had no understanding of how serious the position was.

(b) Study Sources A and B. Source B shows a different attitude to events in Petrograd to that shown in Source A. Use the sources, and your own knowledge, to explain the differences. (6)

Examiner's tip This question is not just asking you to explain how these two sources differ in their attitudes towards events in Petrograd, but to explain why they differ. You should explain that the situation had got worse between February and March and that this partly explains the differences, but that the main reason is to be found by examining the attitudes and motives of the two authors, the Tsarina and Rodzianko. The following answer covers all of these aspects of the question very well.

The Tsarina in Source A does not take the unrest very seriously but Rodzianko in Source B does. One of the reasons for this difference is that the Tsarina was writing in February but Source B was written in March when the situation had become desperate. In February most of the demonstrations were for food but by March the demonstrations were turning political and were criticising the Tsar. Source B mentions the demands of the peasants about land. These demands had been building up for a long time, while in Source A the demonstration is on the spur of the moment. So there is a difference in attitude because the situation in March was more serious. Also, the Tsarina was out of touch with the feelings of ordinary people. This is shown by her reliance on Rasputin and the fact that she sacked the most able ministers. She doesn't understand the people are desperate. Rodzianko was an elected member of the Duma. The Duma did realise how bad the situation was and were demanding reforms. In Source B Rodzianko is trying to argue that there must be reforms.

(c) Study Sources A, B, C and D. Does the evidence of Sources C and D support the version of events given in Source A or in Source B? Explain your answer. (4)

Examiner's tip This question is only worth four marks so do not spend too long on it. Sources C and D support Source B more than they support Source A. It is important that you explain both how they support Source B and how they show less support for Source A. The answer given below is a very full one and would certainly score full marks.

Answers to Unit 3

Answer | Mark

Sources C and D do not support Source A. Source C shows how the strikes were becoming more and more serious. They did not fade away as the Tsarina said they would in Source A. Source D also thinks the situation is very serious because it says nothing can stop the revolution while Source A does not think there will be a revolution. Source D is written at the same time (March) as Source B, and after Source A, and so it is more likely to agree with Source B because the situation did get worse in March.

Source B thinks the situation is serious and both Source C and D agree with this. Source C shows the strikes getting worse and Source D says a revolution is certain. Both Sources C and D can be trusted. Source C is a neutral source and the nurse in Source D has no reason to be biased, so these two sources provide good support for Source B.

(d) Study Sources A, B, C, D, E and F. On 15 March 1917, Tsar Nicholas II abdicated. Use the sources, and your own knowledge, to explain why he did this. (6)

> **Examiner's tip** The instruction in the question to use your own knowledge is very important here. Do not base your answer just on the sources. It is also important to remember that Sources E and F, which have not been used in earlier questions, are included in this question. Look at these two sources carefully for what they tell you about the Tsar's reasons for abdicating. The answer which follows uses knowledge of the topic in two ways. First, to develop the information in the sources, e.g. by explaining how badly the Tsarina governed Russia (develops Source A), and by explaining about the mutiny in the army (develops Source E). Second, by giving information which is not in the sources, e.g. about the Tsar going off in 1915 to command the army.

The Tsar abdicated because of the war, the fact that he was not in Petrograd to control events, and because the Tsarina was in control of the government. All of this led to food shortages and mutiny in the army and demonstrations in Petrograd. By the end of 1914 the war was going badly. The soldiers were not armed properly, they were being beaten by the Germans and millions died. Morale in the army was low. The Tsar then made a terrible mistake. He decided to take control of the army himself. This meant that he was now personally blamed for the way the war was going, and that he had to leave the government in the hands of the Tsarina who had no idea how to govern the country. By 1917 the situation was terrible. The war was still going badly, with the army very unhappy. The soldiers were not fed or paid and the Tsar was blamed. In the cities there was a shortage of food because the transport system had broken down. As Source A shows the Tsarina did not understand how bad things were and did nothing. Source C shows how the strikes got worse in March 1917. The Tsar also refused to believe how bad the situation was as Source F shows. He ordered that the demonstrations be put down by force. But the soldiers in Petrograd refused to fire on the crowds and some mutinied and joined the demonstrations – as Source E shows. This was the crucial event because without the army the Tsar could not stay in control. The Tsar was too far away from Petrograd to do anything and he abdicated.

(e) 'Nicholas II was responsible for his own downfall.' Use the sources, and your own knowledge, to explain whether or not you agree with this interpretation of the events of March 1917. (10)

Answers to Unit 3

Answer	Mark

Examiner's tip In answering this question you must reach a judgement about how far Nicholas II was responsible for his own downfall. You must support your judgement using your knowledge of the topic and the information in the sources. Try not to write a completely one-sided answer which gives Nicholas either all or none of the blame. A sensible answer to this question would attach most, but not quite all of the blame, to Nicholas. The Tsarina, and even Rasputin, were also partly responsible. Finally, as this question is worth ten marks, a developed answer, which supports in detail the points being made, is required. The answer which follows would score very high marks.

I think Nicholas II was mainly responsible for his own downfall. He made a lot of mistakes. His decision in 1915 to take charge of Russia's army in the war was a mistake. He was not a good military commander and he made things worse in the war. It also meant that he would now be directly blamed whenever anything went wrong in the war. The soldiers in the army were badly equipped, they were not led properly and in the winter they suffered very hard conditions. All of this as well as the military defeats turned the soldiers against the Tsar. It was the mutiny of part of the army in 1917 which finally led to his downfall. So his decision to take control of the army was very important. It also meant that he was away from Petrograd, his capital, and was not in control of the important events there. Instead, he left the Tsarina in charge. This was another mistake. The Tsarina governed very badly. She did nothing about the growing unrest and let the very unpopular Rasputin have lots of power. She let the railways collapse which meant that food could not get through to the cities. So in the hard winter of 1916–17 the people in Petrograd were starving and the demonstrations grew. The Tsar was too far away to do anything. In March 1917 the situation got much worse as Source C shows. Source F shows that Rodzianko warned Nicholas how bad things were but he did nothing about it. If the Tsar had returned straight away he might have been able to get the situation under control, but he left it too late. Parts of the army in Petrograd mutinied when they were ordered to attack the demonstrators. With the loss of the support of the army the Tsar was finished. At last he did try and get back, but the railway workers refused to let him back into the city because he was so unpopular.

So there were other reasons like the Tsarina, Rasputin, the failures in the war, and the mutiny of the army but they were all caused by Nicholas II in the first place so he must take most of the blame.

2 In November 1917 the Bolsheviks seized power. In the elections which followed, the Bolsheviks gained only about a quarter of the votes.
Why, then, were the Bolsheviks still in power by the end of 1921? (12)

Examiner's tip The question sets you a problem. After the November 1917 revolution, the Bolsheviks did not have the support of the majority of the Russian people. So how could they keep power? As with any other question which asks 'Why?' something happened, your answer will have to consider many possible causes. Events in history never have a single cause. There are always long-term or conditional causes, which you can use to explain what made it possible for an event to occur, and short-term or contingent causes, which explain how and why that particular event occurred when it did. Constructing an answer which shows the importance of different reasons, and how these reasons acted together to produce the end result – the survival of the Bolsheviks in power – is what you must do to score a high mark. This example shows you how.

Answers to Unit 3

Answer	Mark

The reason why the Bolsheviks were still in power by the end of 1921 is that they were the victors in the Russian Civil War. The real question, then, is why were the Bolsheviks able to win this war?

The Bolsheviks seized power in November 1917. By that time the authority of the Provisional Government had crumbled away. The Bolsheviks had support amongst the industrial workers and the armed forces. Their propaganda, using the slogan 'Peace, Bread, Land', was very effective. It's true that they did not gain a majority of votes in the elections for the Assembly which met in January 1918. But it's also true that the other parties were incapable of uniting and ruling Russia. The Bolsheviks were better organised and better led than any of the other parties, and could probably have seized power earlier than they did. The votes in the election were not a true reflection of which party was the most powerful.

The Bolsheviks promised peace, and in 1918 they signed the Treaty of Brest-Litovsk with the Germans. Lenin knew that he had to have peace at any price. Defeat in the war had destroyed the Tsar and the Provisional Government. By making peace Lenin won the support of the soldiers and sailors who would then fight for the Bolshevik revolution.

When the Civil War broke out, the Bolsheviks had many advantages. They were the government, and controlled Moscow and Petrograd. The Whites were divided, united only in their opposition to the Bolsheviks. They never co-ordinated their efforts against the Bolsheviks. They consisted of monarchists and middle-class groups who were hated by most Russians. Although they were helped by troops sent by Britain, France, Japan and the USA, this intervention by foreigners made them seem unpatriotic. However, at the start of the Civil War, the threat to the Bolsheviks seemed great. They had no proper army, and they controlled only a small area of the country. It was the efforts of Trotsky in creating the Red Army which enabled the Bolsheviks to deal with the Whites. However, the Bolsheviks were also prepared to be ruthless. The Cheka was set up to use terror against all their opponents. War Communism was introduced to take control of industry and to force the peasants to release stores of food for the industrial workers. Once the Bolsheviks were sufficiently organised, they were bound to beat their divided opponents, which explains why they were still in power by 1921.

To sum up, the real reason why the Bolsheviks were able to win the Civil War was what had brought them to power in the first place. Defeat in the First World War had discredited all the other parties. The Russian people had lost faith in the Tsar and the middle classes, and this left the way open for a determined revolutionary group to seize power. The Bolsheviks had good leaders who were ruthless and organised enough to seize power and keep power, particularly as all their opponents were weak and divided.

3 (a) What changes did Stalin introduce in agriculture? (4)

> **Examiner's tip** The main change Stalin made to agriculture was, of course, collectivisation. However it will not be enough to secure the four marks simply to say this. You need to identify some of the main aspects of collectivisation. The following answer makes four points and this would score the full four marks. The four points are identified.

Answers to Unit 3

Answer	Mark

Stalin introduced collective farms. This was when the farmers put their individual plots together to form a collective farm (1). The farm would be run by a committee (2). The peasants would work together and share everything, including the farm produce (3). The government would provide machinery like tractors in return for buying the produce at a low price (4).

(b) Why did he make these changes in agriculture? (6)

> **Examiner's tip**
> In answering this question you need to explain two things. First, what was wrong with the old system of farming? Second, what did Stalin think were the advantages of the new system? If you can, try and explain at least two reasons for each of these. Remember, do not just mention advantages and disadvantages, but explain them. The answer which follows first explains the disadvantages of the old system, and then goes on to explain what Stalin saw as the advantages of collectivisation.

Stalin introduced collectivisation because farming was very backward. Most farms were very small and the peasants poor. This meant they could not afford new machinery and did not know about new methods of farming. This kept the production of farms down. Also, most peasants were only interested in growing enough for their families with a small surplus to buy other things with. They were not interested in mass producing food for the rest of the country.

Collectivisation meant that new machinery and new methods could be introduced. Machinery meant fewer workers were needed and so more men could go and work in the growing factories. The new farms could mass produce food and this could be controlled by the government to match the country's needs. Also collectivisation destroyed the kulaks who were anti-communist.

(c) Stalin made changes both in industry and in agriculture. Which were the more important – the industrial or the agricultural changes? Explain your answer. (10)

> **Examiner's tip**
> You would score a reasonably high mark (7 or 8 out of 10) if you could explain why the changes in one area were more important, and the changes in the other area less important. But to achieve very high marks you should explain how the changes in industry and agriculture were linked. The changes in agriculture were made to enable industry to change and develop. You can see how to do this in the answer which follows. As you can see from this answer you need to explain this in some detail and not just state it. The question is worth ten marks!

It is difficult to say that one was more important than the other because the changes in agriculture were linked with the changes in industry. Both were needed to make Russia a modern and powerful state. Industry could not be developed without agriculture being improved. Improving industry also helped agriculture.

Stalin wanted to develop Russia's industry because Russia was a long way behind countries like the USA. This meant Russia depended on the West for industrial goods which put Russia in a weak position. Stalin wanted Russia to make her own goods, including armaments, to make her strong. Five-Year Plans were put into operation to increase the production of coal, iron, steel and electricity. For this many more workers were needed. This could come from the farms if agriculture was mechanised with machines like tractors and fewer workers were needed there. Hundreds of thousands of workers were moved from farms to industry. These industrial workers had to be fed. Again it was the improvements in agriculture which increased food production which produced the food to

Answers to Unit 3

Answer	Mark

feed the millions of industrial workers. Without this industry would not have been developed.

It also worked the other way round. Developments in industry helped agriculture. This was because industry produced thousands of farm machines like tractors. Without these the farms would not have been mechanised and food production would not have been increased. So both industrial and agricultural changes were important. They depended on each other.

4 THE UNITED STATES, 1919–41

Answer	Mark

1 (a) Study Source A. What can you learn from Source A about the state of the US economy in 1928? (4)

Examiner's tip This is a straightforward comprehension question. Although it is taken from a speech by the President, there is no need to doubt the accuracy of what he says. Weaker answers will simply repeat or paraphrase the source. Better answers, like the example below, will be able to make inferences from the source about the state of the US economy, and set these inferences into the context of the 1920s 'boom'.

Source A shows that the economy was very prosperous. It says that the American economy is doing better than ever before. Hoover as President is obviously bound to make the situation sound good, but it's true that there was a boom in the 1920s and this is what Hoover is describing.

(b) Study Sources A and B. Source B shows a different view of the situation in the US to that in Source A. Use the sources and your own knowledge to explain these differences. (6)

Examiner's tip To explain the differences, first you have to identify them. Source B is pointing out that not everyone shared in the 1920s boom. This is true, but you would not expect Hoover in his speech to want to point it out. In other words, Source A gives a politician's view of the performance of the American economy, and Source B is more concerned with giving a balanced picture. However, note that Source B does not contradict Source A. The writer of Source B would not have disagreed with the claims in Source A. Source A is the truth, but it's not the whole truth. A good answer will explain all this.

The difference between these two sources is simply that Source B identifies that the boom did not benefit everyone. Both sources agree that there was prosperity, but Source A is a positive message being given by a politician, and Source B is a historian's account looking back with the benefit of hindsight. The historian wants to give a balanced judgement about the American economy, and so points out that there were weaknesses, like farming which was in a slump long before the depression hit. But he's not saying there was no boom – it's not that he disagrees with Hoover, it's just that he's making a different point. Hoover probably wants to make his Party look good because they've been in charge whilst America's economy has boomed, so he's not going to point out all the bad things which they haven't solved.

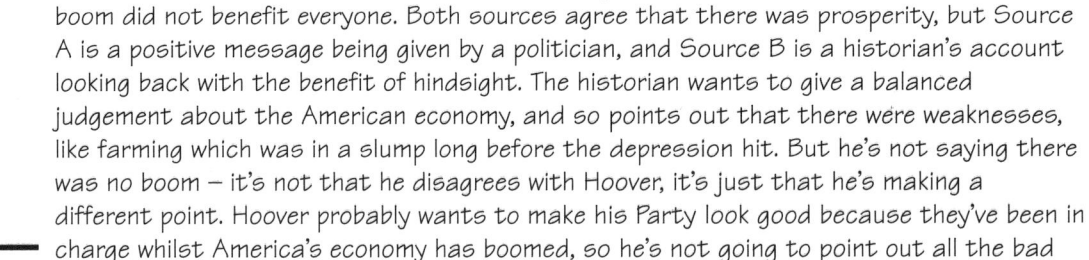

Answers to Unit 4

Answer	Mark

(c) Study Sources A, B, C and D. Does the evidence of Sources C and D support the view given by Source A or in Source B? Explain your answer. (4)

> **Examiner's tip** The small number of marks available for this question is an indication that the task is not a particularly complex one. Source C shows the rapid increase in the production of consumer goods that occurred during the 1920s boom. Source D shows that the residents of this Californian town owned a fair number of cars. Of course, Source D might not show a typical town – California had more than its fair share of the boom – but Source C indicates that there were plenty of new cars to go round. Matching Sources C and D to Source A will provide support for Hoover's view of the American economy in the 1920s. Better answers will realise, however, that what Source B says is not necessarily inconsistent with the other three sources.

Sources C and D seem to support Source A. Hoover's speech is about how the American economy is booming. Source C shows how much production increased between 1920 and 1929, so obviously Hoover was not making the boom up! Source D gives evidence of what the boom meant to ordinary Americans because it shows the main street of a town in California, and there are lots of cars lined up, so obviously lots of people could afford to buy them, and it looks as if there has been lots of new building. However, this is not disputed by Source B. The historian agrees there was a boom, it's just that it did not benefit everyone. Sources C and D illustrate the boom, but Source B wants to make the point that there were groups like farmers for whom the 1920s were not good years. Source C is about industrial production, so it does not tell you anything about farmers.

(d) Study Sources E and F. The boom ended very suddenly in October 1929. Use the sources and your own knowledge to explain why this happened. (6)

> **Examiner's tip** The sources offer information which you can use in your answer, but the question is worded in such a way that it is also acceptable to bring in knowledge that is not in the sources. Answers which identify reasons both from the sources and from background knowledge will score highly.

The sources deal with events in 1929. In fact the causes of the Crash go back further than that. The American economy was not as healthy as most people thought. Some sectors of the economy such as agriculture were in depression long before 1929. Industry was making more than people could buy, which began to push prices down. Profits were falling. But the value of shares was not falling in line with the real economy. People had got used to the idea that the value of shares always went up, so they borrowed money to buy shares. This was fine as long as the shares didn't go down. Sources E and F describe what happened in 1929 when people suddenly lost confidence in the price of shares. Panic selling hit the stock exchange on Wall Street. Billions of dollars were lost as people rushed to sell their shares. Everyone now believed that if they did not sell their shares immediately, they would lose even more money. The price of shares slumped. All the people who had borrowed money to buy shares were ruined as they could not pay their debts.

So much money was lost, and so many people and businesses were made bankrupt, that the economy went from boom to bust almost overnight. As people were made unemployed, so they could not afford to buy the goods that industry made, so industry made less, so more people were made unemployed, and so on. The Wall Street Crash brought the boom to a sudden end.

Answers to Unit 4

Answer	Mark

(e) 'The depression was caused by central government's policy of leaving business alone.' Use the sources and your own knowledge to explain whether or not you agree with this statement. (10)

> **Examiner's tip** The sources do not tell you anything about the Republican government's policies towards business, so you will have to use your own knowledge for this. However, the sources do give some other possible causes of the depression. You need to consider first the evidence which supports the hypothesis that it was Hoover's policy that was to blame, and then the evidence that it was not, before reaching your conclusion.

Hoover, like all Republicans, believed in the economic policy of 'laissez faire'. This meant that government should not interfere in industry and business. He believed that it was the job of businessmen to create prosperity, and that politicians should leave them alone to get on with it. This was fine during the 1920s. The economy was booming, and everyone was happy. The politicians could get the credit just by doing nothing. However, after the shock of the Wall Street Crash it was a different matter. Then people looked to the government for help. Actually Hoover did try to take some steps, like cutting taxes, which he hoped would help industry recover. But he did not do enough. He did not really believe that government could solve what was an economic problem. This was why people were so ready to turn to Roosevelt and his idea of a 'New Deal'.

However, although Hoover can be blamed for not doing enough once the Crash had occurred, this is not the same as blaming him for causing the Crash. The sources give some evidence on why that happened. Source B says that the boom did not benefit everyone, and that most of the wealth was in the hands of a small number of people. This shows that prosperity was not as widespread as many thought. Source C shows how rapidly production increased during the 1920s. Sooner or later people just wouldn't be able to buy any more. Sources E and F show that speculation on the stock market was a major cause of the Crash. The value of shares was much too high, so the stock market could crash the moment people lost confidence. This happened in October 1929. So whatever government policy was, there were plenty of other reasons why a depression hit the USA.

Really the depression was caused by a financial crash, not by the economy being seriously weak, although there were some weaknesses like agriculture. The stock market crash led to bankruptcies and unemployment, which completely undermined the economy and caused the depression. Hoover's policies to cope with the Crash were inadequate, but you can't really blame him for causing the depression except that the policy of 'laissez faire' meant that government did nothing to try and control the boom and speculation that existed before the Crash.

2 (a) What was an 'assembly line'? (4)

> **Examiner's tip** There are only four marks for this question and so just three or four lines will be enough. What is important is to avoid a general answer and to mention some specific points which characterise an assembly line. The answer below makes four specific points and would gain full marks. Each point is identified for you in the answer.

The assembly line was part of mass production (1). It was introduced by Henry Ford in his car factories (2). The work was brought by conveyor belts to the workers (3). Each worker only had one task. The conveyor belt then took the car on to the next worker who did the next job (4).

Answers to Unit 4

Answer	Mark

(b) Why was prohibition repealed in 1933? (6)

Examiner's tip It is important to do two things in your answer. First, you need to explain why prohibition failed. Second, you need to explain why it was repealed in 1933. In other words you need to explain both long-term and short-term reasons. It is also important not just to mention the reasons but to explain how they led to repeal of prohibition. The answer which follows does all of this. It starts with long-term reasons and then moves on to explain why it was repealed in 1933. This answer would achieve full marks.

Prohibition was repealed because it was a failure. It was introduced in 1920 when the making and selling of alcohol was banned. This was to stop drunkenness and prevent men from spending all their wages on drink when their families went hungry. It failed because criminal gangs began to organise the making and selling of alcohol. Men like Al Capone made a fortune from bootlegging. They also ran gambling and prostitution. People did not stop drinking. They went to speakeasies for illegal drink. The gangs fought each other for control. All this led to much more crime, the gangsters bribed the police and many ordinary people were turned into criminals. The police could not enforce prohibition because people found all kinds of ways of getting round it. Most people did not even regard the bootleggers as criminals. The government and the police could not stop the whole of America from drinking. All of this made prohibition very unpopular and the pressure for its repeal was building up all the time. The reason why it was repealed in particular was that Roosevelt promised in his election campaign for president in 1932 to repeal it. He saw that this would be a very popular move. When he became President in 1933 he repealed prohibition.

(c) The following were features of American society in the 1920s:
   (i) prohibition;
   (ii) motor cars;
   (iii) the cinema.
Which of these was the most important in changing the lives of American people? Explain your answer, referring to (i), (ii) and (iii). (10)

Examiner's tip To achieve high marks for this question it is important to explain the role of all three features in the list. Try not to write about each one separately and you must not simply write about the one you think is the most important. There are two ways of scoring a high mark. The first is to compare the importance of the three features in changing the lives of the American people. The second is to show how they were all essential and were all linked with each other. In this particular question it makes sense to compare the importance of the features because prohibition is obviously less important than the other two. The answer below does this very well.

In the 1920s American society was changing very fast in all kinds of ways. The one factor in the list which did not contribute to this was prohibition. Prohibition was passed to uphold old values and the traditional way of life – hard work, saving money and respect for the family and God. So prohibition was introduced to keep things the same not to change them. This is why prohibition failed. It was trying to keep things the same in a time of great change. In 1933 prohibition was abolished. The other two did bring about lots of change. Many more people could buy a car now that Ford was mass producing them. This meant that people became more mobile. They were not trapped in their own communities any more. People took holidays for the first time in their lives and new roads – freeways

Answers to Unit 4

Answer	Mark

and inter-states – began to spread across America. The cinema also changed things. Hollywood produced films which a lot of people saw as immoral. But these films, which could be seen right across the country, gradually changed people's attitudes towards sex. Young people began to copy the film stars rather than their parents. So the cinema and the car did change American society, prohibition did not.

3 (a) Source A shows one of the President's methods of trying to deal with the Depression. Use your own knowledge to explain the cartoon. (5)

> **Examiner's tip** It is important that you use your knowledge of the topic in answering this question, and that you clearly show this knowledge in your answer. The aspects of this cartoon which could be explained are: the use of the radio and why the radio was used; the reference to 'his friends' at the top of the cartoon, and the fact that this cartoon is obviously one of Roosevelt's 'Fireside Chats'. Explaining two of these three points could score full marks. The answer given below explains two of them and would score full marks.

This cartoon shows President Roosevelt speaking to the American people on the radio in one of his fireside chats. In these chats he told everyone what he was planning to do. People felt as if he was speaking to them personally and it boosted their confidence. After one of these chats people stopped taking their money out of the banks. Everyone had a radio and this let Roosevelt speak directly to people in their own homes. He spoke in a friendly way and the chats did a lot to make people believe something was being done about the Depression. This boost in confidence was very important.

(b) Study Source B.
(i) What information does Source B give to explain why the New Deal was introduced? (3)

> **Examiner's tip** There are only 3 marks for this question so a brief answer will be enough. Make sure you take the main points from Source B, e.g. unemployment, fear, the need for government action. The answer below provides a brief explanation of each point and would receive full marks.

This source tells us about the problems facing America which made the New Deal necessary. People were afraid because of the Depression and something had to be done to get rid of their fear and bring back confidence. Problems, like unemployment, were so enormous that only the government was powerful enough to do something about it.

(ii) Use your own knowledge to say whether the source fully explains why the New Deal was introduced. (3)

> **Examiner's tip** Again, there are only three marks so do not launch into a detailed explanation of the reasons for the New Deal. Full marks can be scored either by explaining the source, e.g. by explaining why unemployment was so high, or by giving other reasons why the New Deal was introduced which are not in the source. The answer below adopts the second approach by mentioning other reasons such as bank failures and problems in agriculture.

The source gives some but not all of the reasons why the New Deal was introduced. There was a lot of unemployment but there were other reasons. Farmers were struggling because of a drought and because of falling food prices. Many were ruined. Also, many banks collapsed and people lost all their savings.

Answers to Unit 4

Answer	Mark

(c) Study Sources C and D.
(i) What different interpretations of the effects of the New Deal are given in Sources C and D? (3)

> **Examiner's tip** This is a fairly straightforward question. Source C is obviously claiming that the New Deal was a success while Source D claims that it made the situation worse. In your answer make sure that you support these points with examples from both sources (as the answer given below does).

Source C says that the New Deal was a success because it gave people confidence and fresh ideas, but Source D says the opposite. It claims that it made things worse because people were over-protected and under the power of the President. This means they were less able to look after themselves.

(ii) Use your own knowledge to explain why the views presented in the two sources are different. (3)

> **Examiner's tip** This question is asking you to explain not how the two sources differ, but why they differ. The first thing to do is to look at where the sources come from and when they were written. Source D was written at the time of the New Deal before it was clear how well it was working, and is written by a Republican who would oppose it. Make sure you explain why a Republican would be against the New Deal. Source C is written by a historian in the 1980s and he is able to look back and know what the results of the New Deal were. The answer which follows explains these points well and would score full marks. What you must not do is just state that one source was written today while the other was written at the time. This does not, by itself, explain why the sources differ.

The views are different because Source D was written by a Republican supporter at the time of the New Deal. At that time the idea of governments interfering like this was new and many people in America were worried about it. They did not know what the results would be. Also he is a Republican supporter and Republicans were against government intervention. They thought that people would be stronger if they had to look after themselves without government help. This is why Source D is against the New Deal. Source C was written by a historian fairly recently. He knows what the results of the New Deal were and knows that it did help people.

(d) Study Source E. 'The New Deal achieved its aim: the American people had been "put to work".' Use your own knowledge to explain whether you agree or disagree with this statement. (8)

> **Examiner's tip** The instruction in the question to 'use your own knowledge' is very important here. Also note that there are 8 marks for this question so more explanation is required.
> If you just use Source E you will decide that that the New Deal did put people back to work because unemployment fell. However, if you use your knowledge alongside Source E you will be able to: briefly explain how Roosevelt's measures did put many people back to work; explain that unemployment went up again in 1938 and that the drop in unemployment after 1938 was due to the Second World War, and finally explain that there were some groups in society such as blacks and women who were not helped much by the New Deal. The answer which follows does all of this and would score full marks.

Answers to Unit 4

Answer	Mark

The New Deal did put many people back to work. The Works Progress Administration organised projects like building roads and public buildings. People were also employed in building dams for the Tennessee Valley Authority. All of this led to a fall in unemployment between 1933 and 1937 as Source E shows. But unemployment then went up again. This was because in 1938 Roosevelt laid off many workers employed by the Works Progress Administration because the government was spending too much money. Unemployment falls again after 1938 not because of the New Deal but because of the Second World War which created many new jobs in America. Also, the New Deal did not really find many new jobs for women or for blacks. Most of the people who got jobs under the WPA were men and blacks were still discriminated against when they went for jobs. So overall the New Deal did not get everyone back to work.

(e) What measures did Roosevelt introduce in the 1930s to create employment? How successful were they? (15)

> **Examiner's tip** This question is worth fifteen marks and the length and detail of your answer should reflect this. The answer given below will give you some guidance on this. Whatever you do, do not spend so long on the earlier questions that you do not have enough time to write a proper answer to this question. It carries nearly as many marks as questions (a) to (c) added together!
> It is important to write about specific measures such as the Civilian Conservation Corps and explain how they worked. Other measures include the Works Progress Administration, the National Recovery Administration, the Tennessee Valley Authority, and the Agricultural Adjustment Act. You will not be expected to write about all of these but you should be able to cover at least three of them (the first three mentioned are the most important). However, do not ignore the second part of the question. If you just answer the first part, the most detailed answer will get no more than ten out of fifteen. It is far better to devote about half of your answer to explaining how successful Roosevelt's measures were. You should cover the arguments both in favour of, and against, the New Deal. The answer given below would score very high marks. See if you can identify where it covers the various points mentioned above.

When Roosevelt became President he had a very different approach to the Depression from Hoover. Hoover believed in people sorting out their own problems. Roosevelt believed the government had to do something to give them confidence and help them. He planned to create jobs by spending money on public works schemes. People would then have money to buy goods and this would get the economy going again. He introduced the Civilian Conservation Corps for young men. They planted trees to stop soil erosion and did other jobs and were given monthly wages. The Works Progress Administration employed people to build schools, hospitals and roads. The Tennessee Valley Authority also created lots of jobs. He also gave people confidence through his fireside chats.

These schemes were successful. 8 million people were employed by the WPA and 2.75 million people by the CCC. However nearly all of these were men, and women were found few jobs. But these measures did give the American people their confidence back and industry across America began to recover. Unemployment fell until 1938 when it started to go up again because the WPA was cut back. Roosevelt's measures did help to put people back into work but the Second World War was also very important. American industry produced hundreds of thousands of tanks, planes and guns. The war broke out just as unemployment was beginning to go up again and it was the war not the New Deal which helped to get the figures down at the end of the 30s. The Depression in America was so

Answers to Unit 5

Answer	Mark

enormous that the New Deal could not bring about a recovery by itself. By 1940 America was still not producing as many goods as she had been in 1929, but by 1945 she was producing double the goods of 1929. This shows the importance of the war. It finished the job which the New Deal started.

5 EVENTS IN THE 1930s LEADING TO THE SECOND WORLD WAR

Answer	Mark

1 Study Source A. (a) Describe the ways in which Germany broke the terms of the Treaty of Versailles in the period 1935–8. (8)

Examiner's tip Hitler broke the Treaty in several different ways during these years; his rearmament programme, including an airforce and a navy, remilitarising the Rhineland, and the Anschluss. Given that eight marks are available, it is worth your while to put down as many different ways as you can remember, and to give detail on them. The following answer would be good enough to earn full marks.

In 1935 Hitler was able to break all the limitations that the Treaty had put on Germany's armed forces. Hitler announced that he had created an airforce (the Luftwaffe), he also announced a programme of rearmament including conscription, and finally he signed the Anglo-German naval treaty that allowed him to have a navy 35% the size of Britain's, but with as many submarines as Britain. In 1936 he marched his troops into the Rhineland and remilitarised it. This was the first time he had ignored the territorial terms of the Treaty, and was an enormous gamble, but Britain and France did nothing but protest. In 1938 came the Anschluss with Austria. Hitler had deliberately undermined the Austrian government by encouraging the Austrian Nazis, and when the Austrian Chancellor called a referendum on whether or not Anschluss should occur, Hitler simply invaded Austria and took it over. This was forbidden in the Treaty, but again, Britain and France made no effort to stop him.

(b) 'The Czech people welcomed the arrival of German troops in Prague.' Does Source A support this view? Explain your answer. (4)

Examiner's tip Are the people crying because they are happy or because they are sad? The only way you can know this is by using your knowledge of the topic. The Czechs had been abandoned six months earlier by Britain and France in the Munich Agreement; their country was being taken over against their will. It is reasonable to assume they were crying because they were sad. So why were they giving the Nazi salute? We can only guess that they were doing it because they were forced to, or because they were frightened not to. So answers which are based on the idea that Source A supports the idea that the Czechs welcomed the German invasion, because it shows them giving the Nazi salute, or weeping tears of joy, are showing lack of awareness of the historical context in which the picture was taken. The best answers will try to explain the apparent inconsistency between the Nazi salute and the people crying. There are different ways of doing this. You could argue that Source A is Nazi propaganda taken to show the Czechs weeping tears of joy because of the German invasion; in other words, you would be doubting the reliability of Source A as evidence on Czech reactions. Or you could accept that the source is reliable, showing the distress of the Czechs, but explaining why they had to salute. The following example takes the second of these options.

Answers to Unit 5

Answer — **Mark**

Source A does not support the idea that the Czechs welcomed the German invasion of their country. You can see some of the people crying. This is because they are so distressed by what is happening. They don't want their country to be invaded. They had been abandoned by Britain and France, and they know their country is defenceless. They know that if they don't give the Nazi salute, they will be in danger. Maybe they have been ordered to salute by the Germans, but they still can't hide their true feelings. So in fact Source A supports the view that the Czechs did NOT welcome the Germans.

(c) In September 1938 Britain and France were ready to make an agreement with Germany. In September 1939 Britain and France declared war on Germany. Explain why this change came about. (8)

> **Examiner's tip** In September 1938 Britain, France, Italy and Germany signed the Munich agreement which allowed Hitler to take over the Sudetenland. War broke out in September 1939 over the German invasion of Poland. This question is asking you to explain why Britain and France were prepared to abandon Czechoslovakia in 1938, but not Poland in 1939. As with all other 'Why?' questions, build your answer up by discussing the different reasons for this change of policy, and by showing how these reasons were inter-linked.

By making the Munich agreement, Britain and France showed that they hoped they could appease Hitler – avoid war by giving him what he wanted. Hitler soon showed that this was not to be the case. The Munich agreement left Czechoslovakia defenceless, and in March 1939 Hitler occupied the rest of it. A week later he sent his troops into Memel. Britain and France could no longer fool themselves that Hitler would keep his word. Instead they tried to warn him against further aggression by guaranteeing the independence of Poland, Rumania and Greece. Britain and France were also now rearming at a rapid rate, in readiness for a war which looked ever more likely. So when a new crisis developed in the summer of 1939 over Poland, the attitude of Britain and France was totally different from what it had been a year earlier. They knew that they could do no more to help Poland than they could have done to help Czechoslovakia, but they realised now that Hitler would have to be stopped. They accepted that if Poland was invaded, they would have to declare war on Germany; they just hoped it wouldn't happen. Hitler called their bluff, and invaded Poland, having previously agreed with Stalin a non-aggression pact. Britain and France had no choice but to go to war.

What caused the change in policy from 1938 to 1939 was the failure of appeasement. Once Hitler showed that he would not stop his aggression, and that he would ignore the terms of the Munich agreement, Britain and France had to prepare for war. If Hitler ignored these preparations, then there would be war. The invasion of Czechoslovakia in March 1939 sparked off a chain of events which led to war in September.

Answers to Unit 6

6 THE COLD WAR

Answer	Mark

1 (a)(i) What was meant by the Iron Curtain? (2)

> **Examiner's tip** All that is required here is a definition of the term 'Iron Curtain' in its historical context. The following example would certainly be enough for the two marks.

The 'Iron Curtain' was the boundary between Communist and non-Communist nations in Europe in the years after the Second World War. Churchill was one of the first people to use the term. In 1946 he made a speech in which he said, 'From Stettin in the Baltic to Trieste in the Adriatic, an Iron Curtain has descended upon the Continent.'

(ii) Give ONE reason why an Iron Curtain appeared in Europe in the years after the Second World War. (3)

> **Examiner's tip** The fact that three marks are available indicates that simply giving a reason, for example 'To prevent contact between East and West', is not going to be enough to earn full marks. You will need also to explain your reason, and give some detail about it, as in the following example.

The purpose of the Iron Curtain was to prevent people in the Communist East having contact with people in the capitalist West. The Soviet Union was afraid that such contacts would make people in the East dissatisfied and more likely to rebel against Soviet domination. If they had no contact with the West, the people in the East would be more likely to believe Soviet propaganda.

(iii) Explain the effects that the Iron Curtain had upon Europe in the years to 1955. (6)

> **Examiner's tip** This question is about the consequences of the existence of the Iron Curtain – what difference did it make? It was created because of the Cold War – the increasing tension between the Communist East and the Democratic West. How did it add to this tension? An answer which shows awareness of events between 1946 and 1955, and can link these to the existence of the Iron Curtain, will score well. The following example shows how to do this.

The Iron Curtain was the physical boundary between the Communists and the West. It was very difficult for those on one side to know what was happening on the other side. This added to the mistrust and fear that the two sides felt. It made it easy for both sides to use misleading propaganda about each other. In these conditions the Cold War developed. When the Americans proposed Marshall Aid, the Soviet Union made sure all the Eastern countries rejected it. Naturally, the countries in Western Europe accepted it. In 1948 the Russians tried to push the West out of Berlin, the only area east of the Iron Curtain in the West's hands. The West responded with an airlift to demonstrate that they would not give in to Russian aggression. The idea of East and West being two separate sides was eventually recognised when first NATO and then the Warsaw Pact were established. The Iron Curtain made all these developments easier to happen.

(iv) Why was there a blockade of Berlin from 1948 to 1949? (6)

Answers to Unit 6

Answer	Mark

> **Examiner's tip** As always with 'Why?' questions, look for multiple causes, and show how they worked together to produce the stated outcome. For six marks, this need not be too detailed. Three or four causes, explained fully, will be enough to gain full marks, as in this example.

The Berlin Blockade arose over disagreements between the USSR and the West over how to run their zones of occupation in Germany. The West wanted to get Germany back on its feet, and the Soviet Union wanted to keep it weak. Britain and the USA made one economic unit out of their zones, and announced they were going to set up a new currency for Germany. The USSR refused to take part in this, and to show their disapproval began to disrupt communications with West Berlin. By June 1948 they had cut West Berlin off entirely. This was the start of the blockade.

Of course, if the USSR and the West had trusted each other more, the quarrel over Germany probably would not have become so serious. You could say, then, that the blockade was caused by the Cold War. Probably the USSR thought they could force the West out of Berlin without having to fight. West Berlin was like an island of freedom behind the Iron Curtain, and the USSR would want to take it over if they could.

The blockade lasted so long because the West refused to give in. They organised an airlift which kept West Berlin supplied. The USSR thought they could starve West Berlin into submission, but they couldn't.

(v) In what ways did the blockade change relations between the superpowers in the years to 1953? (8)

> **Examiner's tip** This is another question about consequences – what did the blockade change? You need to identify changes brought about by the blockade, and show how the blockade brought these changes about. The more detail you can include to support your analysis, the better.

The most important result of the blockade was that it settled the question of Germany. Before it the two sides pretended that they were working together to occupy and administer Germany. After it the division of Germany into two was made permanent. The West set up the Federal Republic and the East set up the Democratic Republic. There was no longer any attempt to work together. The blockade was the first major confrontation between the wartime Allies. This marked a new phase in the Cold War. What happened in Germany now became the case for East and West as a whole. The two sides regarded each other as enemies. In 1949 the West set up NATO which was an anti-Communist alliance. The USSR set up Comecon to coordinate the economies of Eastern Europe. In 1955 the USSR set up the Warsaw Pact as a counter to NATO. Between 1949 and Stalin's death in 1953 the Cold War was at its height. The blockade was not the only factor which caused this increase in tension – other events like the Korean War also played a part – but in some ways the blockade was the most important as it marked the point at which the two sides ceased just being suspicious of each other, and became enemies.

(b) (i) Why was the US government concerned about events in Cuba from 1960 to 1962? (10)

Answers to Unit 6

Answer	Mark

> **Examiner's tip** The number of marks indicates that an extended answer is required. The period from 1960 to 1962 spans the years in which Castro's dictatorship in Cuba was established up to the missiles crisis of 1962. A decision you have to take is how much to write on the missiles crisis itself – the question does not guide you clearly on this. In such cases it is better to be safe than sorry, so include it, or at least the causes of the crisis, which, of course, were part of American 'concerns' about Cuba. This example shows you what is required.

Castro came to power in Cuba in 1959. It was not clear whether he was a Communist, but it soon became obvious that he would follow an anti-American policy. Cuba's previous ruler, Batista, was an American ally, and had encouraged American investment. For America it was bad enough that he had been overthrown. To make matters worse, Castro nationalised American businesses and seized their assets. In retaliation the Americans placed a boycott on Cuba's main export, sugar. Cuba faced bankruptcy, but the Soviet Union offered to buy Cuba's sugar instead. Now America faced the threat of having a Soviet ally only 90 miles away. This was hard to accept. US foreign policy has never tolerated the influence of other major powers in the Americas.

The USA now began to plot to overthrow Castro. In April 1961 an invasion of Cuba by Cuban exiles took place. This was known as the Bay of Pigs invasion, and it was backed by the Americans. Unfortunately for them, it was a total failure. All it achieved was to push Castro even more firmly into the arms of the Russians. Castro accepted an offer from the USSR to build missile bases in Cuba. When American spy planes detected these in 1962, a major international crisis developed. The USA would not tolerate the existence of Soviet missiles close enough to the USA that every American city was threatened. Kennedy gave Khrushchev an ultimatum to remove the missiles, and placed a blockade around Cuba. Eventually Khrushchev backed down, but only after the world had seemed on the brink of nuclear war.

(ii) Did the Cuban Missile Crisis change relations between the superpowers? Explain your answer. (15)

> **Examiner's tip** The Crisis did change relations in some ways – for example, the 'hot line' was set up – but you are not going to earn full marks simply for dealing with changes. The question is really asking how much the Crisis changed relations, so you will need to reach a judgement based on analysis of what changed and what did not change. Again, the large number of marks indicates that an extended response is required. This example would score a very high mark.

The Cuban Missile Crisis was so serious that it was bound to change the relationship between the USSR and the USA. Nuclear war had narrowly been avoided. The two countries agreed to establish a 'hot line' – a telephone link so that their leaders could communicate directly with each other in future crises. This was at least a sign that they both recognised that it was better to talk than fight. In 1963 they signed the Test Ban Treaty, which outlawed testing of nuclear weapons in the atmosphere. The USA and the USSR seemed to accept that both countries had a right to exist and to have their own spheres of influence. This was a period of peaceful co-existence.

However, this did not mean that the two countries had become friendly. The basic difference between them – the competition between the Communist and the Capitalist

Answers to Unit 6

Answer	Mark

superpowers – had not been resolved. The 1960s saw many serious international disputes, like the Vietnam War, in which the USA and the USSR were on opposite sides; they simply made sure that they never came into direct confrontation with each other. The arms race continued, with both sides putting together collections of nuclear weapons which could destroy the world many times over. The Cuban Missile Crisis slightly improved the relationship between the two sides, but it did not bring the Cold War to an end.

2 (a) What were the main aims of the United Nations Organisation when it was set up in 1945? (4)

> **Examiner's tip** This question is simply asking you to recall some information. It does not require you to explain or analyse. With only four marks available, you can assume that giving a couple of the main aims of the UNO, and adding some supporting details to each, will be enough to gain all the marks

The main aim of the UNO was to maintain international peace. It could do this by putting together peace-keeping forces from amongst its member states. These forces have served in many parts of the world, keeping apart nations that might otherwise had fought against each other. The UNO also aimed to work for human rights and improving the quality of life for people around the world. Its agencies such as WHO have done a lot of good work, such as fighting disease and promoting educational schemes.

(b) Explain why the United Nations intervened in Korea in 1950. (6)

> **Examiner's tip** There is a difference between identifying reasons why something happened, and explaining those reasons. For example, a reply to this question could be 'Because the North Koreans invaded South Korea'. This identifies a reason, but does not explain it. To do that you might say 'Because the North Koreans invaded South Korea, and the United Nations would not tolerate such aggression'. Any answer, such as the one which follows, which thoroughly explains two or three causes for the UNO's intervention, would score full marks.

A very important reason why the UNO was able to intervene in Korea is that the USSR was absent from the Security Council when it took its vote. If it had been there it would certainly have vetoed any action, but it was temporarily absent because the USA refused to let China join the UNO. However, this does not explain why intervention was necessary. That was because North Korea had invaded South Korea. The North was Communist, and the USA wanted to prevent it taking over the whole country. Rather than having to help South Korea on its own, it preferred to go through the UNO, which condemned the North Koreans as aggressors, and sent United Nations forces to drive them out.

(c) How successful was the United Nations' intervention in Korea? Explain your answer. (10)

> **Examiner's tip** The words 'How successful?' should alert you to the idea that the intervention was successful in some ways, but unsuccessful in others. Your answer should consider both aspects before reaching a conclusion. Good answers will find several ways to judge both success and lack of success.

Answers to Unit 7

Answer	Mark

The purpose of the UN's intervention in Korea was to prevent the North taking over the South. When the UN's forces arrived the North Koreans had captured almost all of the South, but soon they were driven back. This first phase of the war was definitely a success for the UNO.

However, when China saw North Korea, its ally, getting beaten, it joined in the war. The UN had made a big mistake in invading North Korea. They weren't satisfied with simply rescuing the South, they wanted to remove Communism from the North as well. Provoking China into joining the war was guaranteed to prolong the war, and make it a much bigger war than before. The Chinese attack was very successful, and they pushed the UN forces all the way back into South Korea again. Obviously this phase of the war was not a success for the UN.

The war dragged on for nearly three more years. Slowly, the UN regained the parts of South Korea which had been lost. In 1951, MacArthur, the UN Commander, was sacked when he suggested using nuclear weapons against China. By this time the American politicians were ready to settle for a peace based on the boundary between North and South which had existed before the war, but it took two more years before a ceasefire was agreed in 1953. During this time many more people, both civilians and soldiers, were casualties. The UNO had saved South Korea, but had become stuck in a pointless stalemate.

There was no peace treaty, and the two parts of Korea are still bitter enemies, so the UN intervention did not solve the problems of Korea. In this way it was unsuccessful. But it did show that aggression would be resisted, and restore South Korea's territory, which were successes.

7 THE SOVIET INVASION OF CZECHOSLOVAKIA, 1968

Answer	Mark

1 Read Source A. What can you tell about the situation in Czechoslovakia in early 1968 from this source? (6)

Examiner's tip This is a nice straightforward question to begin with. There are two levels at which this question can be answered. First, in reading the source, you will see that it gives you information about what was going on in Czechoslovakia at that time. For instance, you can say that it tells you the Czechs needed education, or flats. Answers at this level are just using comprehension of the source, which is fine in itself, but limited. Watch out for questions which ask what a source tells you. This is not an invitation simply to repeat what the source says. You should also look beneath the surface of this source, and try to work out what it really means. In other words, you should try to make inferences based on your comprehension of the source. A simple inference would be that the Czechs were dissatisfied. The source does not say this in as many words, but it is easy to understand that the person making the speech was not happy about the state of the country. A better kind of inference is where you use your historical knowledge to make inferences about the events of the time. Here you might say that the source tells you that Dubček's reforms had encouraged people to be very critical of Communist rule, otherwise they would not have dared to make speeches like this. The highest marks would be reserved for answers which show the ability to make this kind of inference, and if you can include more than one such inference, so much the better.

Answers to Unit 7

Answer | **Mark**

I can tell that the people of Czechoslovakia were not happy. If they all agree with the person making this speech then they have lots to worry about. Housing and education are no good. This person is even ashamed of the country, because the source talks about the country losing its good reputation. (So far the answer shows comprehension and simple inferences.) You can tell the difference that Dubček's reforms had made in Czechoslovakia by this time. People obviously felt free to criticise what the government had done in the past. In most Communist countries you would not dare to speak as openly as this. So I can also tell that Communism in Czechoslovakia was probably in trouble because the speech is really a criticism of everything Communism has done. You can see this where it says that in twenty years not one problem has been solved – this is the twenty years that the Communists have been in power. (The answer has now made inferences in the specific context of the events of 1968.)

2   Read Source B. How far does this source explain why the Soviet Union invaded Czechoslovakia in 1968? Explain your answer. (8)

> **Examiner's tip**
> The words 'how far?' should always alert you to the need to look at all sides of the question, and to reach a balanced conclusion. Here you are invited to judge first whether or not Source B gives you reasons why the Soviet Union invaded, and then whether these reasons provide a complete explanation. In fact Source B does mention several, closely related reasons why the Soviet Union was unhappy about what was going on in Czechoslovakia: that Czechoslovakia was moving away from Communism ('pushed off the road to socialism'), that this might undermine Communist rule elsewhere ('puts in danger the whole socialist system'), and that Czechoslovakia could not be allowed to break away from Russian domination ('being cut off from the socialist community of countries'). There is no reason to doubt the reliability of this source; even though it was sent to warn the Czechs, the reasons it gives are entirely plausible and fit the facts as we know them. However, you may think that there are other reasons not mentioned in Source B, in which case you can conclude that Source B gives some of the explanation but not all of it. In looking for additional reasons you can use the other sources and your own knowledge. One obvious reason, again related to those given in Source B, is the strategic importance of Czechoslovakia. It had an eastern frontier with Russia, and a western frontier with West Germany and Austria. If Czechoslovakia ceased to be Communist, the Iron Curtain would be broken and the West would have a direct route to attack Russia. Obviously, Russia would not willingly allow this to happen.
> To sum up, the best answers will first identify any reasons for invasion given in Source B, then decide whether these reasons are believable, and finally mention other reasons not given in Source B in order to reach a balanced answer to the question 'How far?'.

Source B was sent as a warning to the Czechs not to think they could split from the other Communist countries and get away with it. It says they are leaving the road of socialism, and that if they do this, then it threatens the other Communist countries because they might do the same. It warns that Russia will not allow Czechoslovakia to stop being Communist. All these are good reasons to invade from the Russian point of view. They had set up the Iron Curtain to protect their own security, and they weren't going to allow countries in Eastern Europe to decide for themselves whether they were going to stay Communist. The reasons given in Source B do really explain why the Soviet Union invaded, but you could add some more detail to explain them better. Czechoslovakia made the Soviet Union particularly nervous because it had a border with West Germany and a border with Russia, so if it stopped being Communist then it would provide a corridor for enemies to attack Russia. Another reason could be that even though Dubček

Answers to Unit 7

Answer	Mark

said he did not want to overthrow Communism, just reform it, the Russians thought he was too weak to control events, and he would end up going much further than he intended.

3 Read Sources C and D. Does Source D prove the Soviet government is lying in Source C? Explain your answer. (9)

> **Examiner's tip** More often than not the reliability of a source is not really an issue. Many sources are written from a particular point of view, but they do not set out deliberately to mislead the reader. With Sources C and D, however, you need to work out who you believe, because both cannot be telling the truth. Source C says that the Czech leaders invited Soviet troops into Czechoslovakia to give assistance, and Source D says the invasion took place without the knowledge of any of the Czech leaders. The question asks whether the Soviet government is lying, so let's consider them first. If Source C is not the truth, then what purpose could the Soviet government have for lying? Obviously they would need an excuse for invading. They would try to convince the other Communist countries, and countries in the rest of the world, that they were only trying to help Czechoslovakia. They wouldn't want to look like the aggressor. How about the Czechs? Would they have any reason to lie? It's hard to think of any – it was their country being invaded, and why would they condemn the invasion as being against international law if they agreed with it? The only doubts you might have about Source D is whether the Communist Party would be in a position to know what the President and Prime Minister had done, but the fact that it is making a radio broadcast is a sign that there was official approval for what was said. Anyway, in Communist states there is little difference between the top members of the Party and the members of the government. The best answers, then, will be those that discuss the reliability of both sources, and use knowledge of the events to explain why each source says what it does, in order to reach a conclusion. It is, of course, impossible to say that Source D proves that Source C is lying, but it makes it very likely.

Source C is just an excuse for invading. It's a kind of propaganda which always happens when nations do something illegal, like when Hitler invaded Poland in 1939. The Russians did not want to look bad in front of the rest of the world. It was a bit humiliating having to invade Czechoslovakia to keep it in line, so they pretend that the Czechs have asked them. Nobody would really believe it, at least not in the West. Maybe they would be so brainwashed in other Communist countries that they would think that the Russians had been invited into Czechoslovakia. Source D is much more credible. You can believe what it says because it is the day after the invasion has started, and yet the broadcast is critical of what the Russians are doing. If it was propaganda it would be agreeing with the invasion. You would have to be brave to say these things because the Russian troops would soon be able to arrest you. So Source D shows up the lies in Source C. It says that the Czech leaders knew nothing of the invasion, but Source C pretends these leaders invited the Russians in. The Czechs have no reason to lie, but the Russians do, so I believe Source D. I suppose you could say that Source D doesn't absolutely prove the Russians are lying because the people making the broadcast might not know everything that had gone on, but that's not likely. It does not make sense that the Czechs would ask for the invasion of their own country, and anyway the Communist Party would know what was going on because it was involved in the government.

4 Study Sources E and G. How similar are these two sources? Explain your answer. (9)

> **Examiner's tip** The words 'How similar?' should alert you to the fact that you are not simply being asked 'What are the similarities between these two sources?' – you must also consider differences. There are several low-level ways of answering this question. You could refer to source type – they are similar because they are both

Answers to Unit 7

Answer	Mark

pictures, or different because one is a photograph and one is a cartoon. This would not get many marks. A little better would be the identification of surface differences in what the sources show — they are similar because they both show Russian soldiers, or different because there is a little girl in one and a man in the other. Again, this would get no more than a couple of marks. Many answers would focus on the events — they are similar because they both concern the Russian invasion of 1968, or different because Source E deals also with the Russian liberation of Czechoslovakia from Germany in 1945. This would earn around half marks. Good answers would interpret the messages of the two sources. This could be done in several ways. One could say that they are similar because they portray the Russians in 1968 as oppressors, but they differ because Source E implies some sympathy for the Russians who were once Czechoslovakia's liberators. The best answers, however, would deal with the issues of why these images were created and who they were created for. The following example first interprets the two sources and then analyses their purpose. It would certainly earn full marks in that it operates at the highest level, and addresses the issue of 'How similar?'.

Source E contrasts the events of 1945 and 1968. In 1945 the Russian army liberated Czechoslovakia from German rule, so the little girl is shown presenting the Russian soldier with flowers. It asks the question why must the young girl (who represents Czechoslovakia) be killed by the Russians in 1968 when she welcomed them in 1945? Source G deals only with the events of 1968, but it, too, seems to be asking the question 'why?'. The man pleading with the Russian soldier is unarmed, which you can see because he has his hands empty, and held out in a gesture which seems to show he does not understand why the Russians have occupied his country.

The sources are similar because they have the same purpose — they are protests about what has happened. They both disagree with the invasion and seem to show that it was unnecessary as the Czechs pose no threat to the Russians. They are both intended to create sympathy for the Czechs. But they do this in different ways because they are intended for different audiences. The street cartoon would probably be pasted onto a wall as a sign of non-violent resistance by the Czechs. Russians who saw it might be persuaded that the Czechs were right, and Czechs who saw it would feel that the Russians weren't just being allowed to get away with the invasion. The photograph is likely to be for a wider, international audience. The photographer has taken this picture to try and sum up the invasion and its consequences in a single image — the Russian military machine against unarmed civilians who only want their freedom.

5 **Study Source F. Does this source show that the Czechs supported Communism or not? Explain your answer.** (8)

Examiner's tip This question requires you to interpret the cartoon. Once you have done this you will be able to judge whether or not the Czechs — or at least the person who drew the cartoon — supported Communism. The fact that it was a street cartoon can be taken to mean that many Czechs would have agreed with it, if not all. In fact, as we shall see, the cartoon lends itself to more than one interpretation, and the best answers will reflect this in the conclusions they reach.
The cartoon is a comment on the events of 1968. The tank in the cartoon is Russian and represents the invasion. Lenin was the hero of the Russian Revolution and the creator of Communism in Russia. The fact that he is weeping can be taken as a sign that he would disagree with the 1968 invasion. The simplest interpretation is that if even Lenin is weeping, the invasion must be wrong. The cartoonist was anti-Russian and therefore does not support Communism. If this interpretation was supported by use of details of the cartoon it would be awarded a reasonable mark.

Answers to Unit 7

Answer	Mark

There is, though, a more subtle answer. You could argue that the cartoonist was sympathetic towards Communist ideas, and shows Lenin weeping because of the tragedy of one Communist nation invading another. In other words, the ideals of Communism have been betrayed by the Russian invasion. This would fit with what the Czech leaders always claimed – that they did not want to overthrow Communism, but just intended to improve or reform it. In other words, they supported Communism, but not the Russian version of it.

I think the cartoon shows that Czech people were sympathetic towards communism, but opposed the Russian invasion. The tank is invading Czechoslovakia and Lenin is crying about it. This shows that the cartoonist was strongly against the Russian invasion, so you could say that it shows an anti-Communist viewpoint because the Russians were the chief Communist power. But why show Lenin crying then? He was the founder of Communism in Russia, so the cartoonist is using him to represent what good Communists should feel. As he is against the invasion then it shows that good Communists could be against the invasion. I think this is what the cartoonist thinks. If he wasn't a Communist then he wouldn't use the picture of Lenin. He opposes the invasion, but doesn't oppose Communism. Of course, you could also think that this street cartoon was intended for Russians to see. Then you could interpret it differently again, and say it could just be mocking the Russians – like saying to them that even your great leader Lenin would think it a bad idea that one Communist country is invading another. Then you couldn't say whether the Czechs supported Communism or not.

6 Study Source H. What was the cartoonist's opinion of Soviet actions towards Czechoslovakia? Explain your answer using details of the cartoon. (8)

Examiner's tip This is a similar question to the previous one. You need to interpret the cartoon using your knowledge of events. There is also a specific instruction to use the details of the cartoon, so you must do this to achieve a good mark. The cartoon is American, so you should not expect it to show much sympathy for the Soviet actions. A crucial point in interpreting the cartoon is to recognise that Brezhnev and Kosygin, the Soviet leaders, are being portrayed as gangsters, and that their intention in setting Dubček's feet in concrete is to dispose of him by dropping him somewhere in deep water. This is a deeply hostile way of portraying the leaders of another country and indicates the cartoonist's disgust at the Soviet actions in Czechoslovakia. A full interpretation of the cartoon would depend on identifying these points. However, even if you missed the gangster reference, it would still be possible to make something of the cartoon. It is, for instance, obvious that Dubček has been captured, and he looks alarmed at being in the hands of the two Soviet leaders. You could tell from this that the cartoonist thinks something nasty might happen to Dubček. The Soviet leaders are shown in an unflattering way, and it is clear that the cartoonist disapproves of what they are doing.
The following answer gives a very full interpretation, using features of the cartoon, and identifies the specific event to which it refers. It would certainly achieve full marks.

The cartoonist was very much against Soviet actions towards Czechoslovakia. You can tell this because of the way he shows the two Soviet leaders. He makes them look like characters out of a film about the Mafia. They are dressed in flashy suits with padded shoulders. They have got Dubček weighted down with concrete and chains and they are about to take him away and drown him. This means that the cartoonist thinks that, by invading Czechoslovakia, the Soviet Union has behaved like a gangster. He virtually

Answers to Unit 7

Answer — **Mark**

accuses the Soviet leaders of wanting to murder Dubček. Of course they did not do this, but they did take him off to Moscow, which is what this cartoon is probably about. The cartoonist probably expected Dubček to disappear and not be seen again.

7 Use all the sources. How far do these sources show that it was not really necessary for the Soviet Union to invade Czechoslovakia in 1968? Explain your answer. (12)

> **Examiner's tip** The task here is to use the sources to test the hypothesis that there was no real need for the Soviet Union to invade Czechoslovakia in 1968 – in other words, that what was happening in Czechoslovakia was not a real threat to the security of the Soviet Union. Do not fall into the trap of writing an essay about the hypothesis, and forgetting all about the sources. You will find evidence in these sources both supporting and conflicting with the hypothesis. You should mention the evidence on both sides. This will help you reach a conclusion to the question 'How far?'. The best answers will be those that do not simply accept the sources at face value, but show an awareness of the need to assess their reliability in relation to the hypothesis before using them. The answer below does this well. Many students will go through each of the sources in turn, commenting on whether it supports the hypothesis or not. You do not have to do this. A better approach is to summarise the evidence you can find which supports the hypothesis, then the evidence against it, before reaching your conclusion. Grouping the evidence in this way makes it far easier for you to keep sight of the argument you are trying to make as an answer to the question. In this set of sources those that are sympathetic towards the Czechs generally give the message that the invasion was not necessary. Those that are from a Soviet perspective provide the counter-arguments. The following example is arranged in this manner, and is very successful in summarising the evidence as a whole, rather than just going through the sources and using them as a checklist.

Whether or not the invasion was really necessary is bound to be an issue over which the Czechs and the Russians would disagree. The Russians would not have invaded unless they believed it necessary. The Czechs claimed all along that they were not threatening the Communist system, so they would see the invasion as unnecessary. The sources reflect this split.

Sources B, C and I are Russian. Leaving aside the fact that Source C is just an excuse for invading, the three sources are consistent in arguing that the Czechs posed a threat to the security of the Communist bloc, and that they could not be allowed to go their own way. We know that this is the attitude the Russians had towards Eastern Europe, and there is no reason to doubt that these sources give a good insight into the reasons why the Soviet Union felt they had to invade Czechoslovakia. The real question is whether their fear of what was happening in Czechoslovakia was justified. There is some evidence from the other sources that it was. We do not know who was making the speech in Source A, or whether many Czechs agreed with it, but it is an indication that Dubček was allowing so much freedom that Communism itself was coming under criticism. This kind of freedom was not allowed anywhere else in the Soviet bloc, and you can see why they would have been alarmed by it. Communism and freedom of speech did not go together well.

Sources D, E, F and G are all from the Czech point of view. They portray the Czechs as innocent and unthreatening. However, at least three of these sources were created with the specific aim of rousing sympathy for what had happened to Czechoslovakia. Sources E, F and G do not attempt to explain why the Russians had invaded, because their purpose is to demonstrate the effects of the invasion. It is hard not to feel sympathy for

Answers to mock examination paper

Answer — **Mark**

a country invaded in this way. The sources seem to show that Czechoslovakia could not possibly be a threat – the little girl with flowers in Source E, the unarmed protester in Source G – and yet the very fact that the Czechs could show the desire for freedom in their protests and street cartoons was threatening to the Russians. The Czechs could try to pretend that they were good Communists, but Source F shows how difficult this was. They ended up using the image of Lenin to show their disapproval of the invasion. But how could they be good Communists if the Russians thought it necessary to invade?

In many ways the most realistic summary is Source H. Although an American comment on the events of 1968, it backs up what Source I says. Portraying the Soviet leaders as gangsters makes it clear that the invasion was about one thing only – Soviet power. Nothing could be allowed to threaten it. Whether Czechoslovakia wanted to remain Communist or not was irrelevant, the Russians would not permit any of the countries in the Eastern bloc to show signs of independence. Source I makes a similar point about the Brezhnev Doctrine – this was the Russians saying 'This is our patch'. Within this area they would decide whether invading their neighbours was necessary or not, and the signs of independence shown by the Czechs in 1968 were ample reason for them to worry.

8 MOCK EXAMINATION PAPER

Answer — **Mark**

1   Study Source A.
   According to Source A, why did the USA introduce the Marshall Plan? (5)

> **Examiner's tip** Remember that you are being asked about what Source A says about the reasons for the USA introducing the Marshall Plan, not about what reasons you can remember. Avoid copying large parts of the source. Read Source A through and make a rough list of all the reasons you can find. Then decide if Source A is suggesting that one reason was more important than the others.
> The first part of the source explains that Truman introduced the Plan to help Europe recover from the war. However, he was not doing this simply to help Europe. The source makes clear that he did not want Europe to become poor because poverty helped Communism to spread. Therefore his real reason for introducing the Plan was to stop Communism from spreading. He also wanted European countries to be strong, so that they could defend themselves, as he did not want the USA to be left on its own to face the Russians. These reasons are still associated with the main idea to stop Communism. It is also worth pointing out that the US Congress only agreed once the Communists took over Czechoslovakia – this was the trigger that persuaded them to agree to the Plan.
> The final paragraph of Source A suggests different reasons and you should make it clear that you understand that Source A is saying that there are differing views about this question. The answer below makes clear that stopping Communism from spreading was the main reason but also explains that there are other views about US motives. It would score five marks.

Source A says that the USA introduced the Marshall Plan to stop Communism from spreading. Truman did not want Communism to spread across Europe. He thought that Communism spread when people were poor and so by helping Europe recover and become rich he was preventing Communism spreading. Helping Europe to become rich would also

Answers to mock examination paper

Answer	Mark

mean that they were strong enough to defend themselves against Communism. This was the main reason for the US. But the short term reason was the Communist takeover of Czechoslovakia. This showed that the threat from Communism was real and forced the US to actually go ahead with the Plan. Source A also says that other people think that the US introduced the Marshall Plan for other reasons like creating markets for American goods to help American industry. So there is no agreement about this question.

2 Study Source B.
   Do you think the cartoonist approved of the Marshall Plan? Explain your
   answer referring to details of the cartoon and your own knowledge. (5)

> **Examiner's tip** To answer this question well you must study the drawings and read the captions in the cartoon carefully. You will not get a very good mark if you simply say that the cartoonist would be against the Marshall Plan because he was Russian. The question does tell you to explain your answer by using details in the cartoon. You must do this. Each drawing shows a figure representing the USA trying to persuade Europeans to rely on the USA rather than providing for themselves. They need not grow maize or build ships because the USA will sell them whatever they want. The last drawing suggests that this will lead to Europe being completely under the control of the USA because they will not even have their own policies. The answer which follows scored full marks because it shows an understanding that the cartoonist is saying the Marshall Plan is a device for the USA to control Europe so he is against it. The answer is supported by examples from the cartoon.

The artist was against the Marshall Plan. In the first picture America is telling Europeans that they needn't grow their own maize because America will provide it. It looks as if America is doing Europe a favour but it isn't really because it is getting control. All the other pictures give a similar message. They are saying that the Marshall Plan looks as if it is helping Europe but really it was to give the USA control over Europe by making Europe dependent on US goods. Europe will have no shipyards of its won and finally in the last picture no policies of its own. The cartoonist is also saying that the Marshall Plan was to help America's industries by turning Europe into a market for them.

3 Study Sources B and C. How far does Source C agree with Source B about the
   Marshall Plan? Explain your answer by referring to details of the two cartoons
   and your own knowledge. (6)

> **Examiner's tip** You will already have decided what Source B thinks of the Marshall Plan. You must now compare this with the opinion given in Source C. Often with comparison questions such as this one the best answer is not straightforward. This is because Source C both agrees and disagrees with Source B! The cartoonist is suggesting that the USA is being very generous towards Europe and is therefore praising the Plan. This makes Source C very different from Source B. However, he also criticises the plan by drawing the US taxpayer complaining that her taxes are going abroad when the money needs to be spent in America for the good of Americans. Although both Source B and Source C are criticising the Plan they are doing so for different reasons and this would be another way to explain both agreement and disagreement. The answer below answers the question this way and was awarded full marks.

Source C is against the Plan. This makes it agree with Source B which is also against the Plan. The cartoonist in Source C is saying that there are many poor taxpayers in America

Answers to mock examination paper

Answer	Mark

who need help but their taxes are being used to help Europe instead. The woman represents a poor taxpayer and she is complaining that the US government is being too generous with her money. However, although both cartoons criticise the Marshall Plan they do so for different reasons. Source C is saying that America was being too generous while Source B is saying the opposite. It is suggesting that the Plan has been designed to help American industries by making Europe into a huge market for American goods and to put Europe under the control of America. So the USA was not being generous at all. The Marshall Plan was to benefit America.

4 Study Sources D and E. Sources D and E agree about the Marshall Plan. Does this mean that they are reliable?
Use your own knowledge to help you explain your answer. **(6)**

Examiner's tip These two sources both claim that the Marshall Plan was designed to place European countries under the control of the USA. They claim that America wants to destroy freedom in Europe and is using the Plan to achieve this. Of course, the fact that they agree does not in itself mean they are are reliable. However, you must go further than simply claiming that they are not reliable because they are from the USSR. There are several elements to a good answer to this question. Firstly, look at where the sources come from, who is speaking, and who they were speaking to. Use your knowledge of the situation in 1947 (the beginning of the Cold War between the USSR and the USA and the attempt by Stalin to control Europe) to explain the possible motives of the USSR spokesmen in these two sources and how this affects the reliability of what they say. The answer below does this very well. Another way of answering the question would be to use your knowledge of the Marshall Plan and the situation in 1947 to check what the two sources claim about the Marshall Plan.

The fact that these two sources agree does not make them reliable. The Cold War between the USSR and the USA had started and these two countries were now enemies. They were fighting for control of Europe. Stalin wanted to get control of Eastern Europe Countries like Hungary and Poland which were already communist and there was a civil war going on in Greece with the US supporting those fighting against communist control. So the speech to the UN in Source D has to be seen in this context. The USSR is trying to turn other countries against America and the Marshall Plan because it wants to control Eastern Europe instead. This means we cannot trust Source D. In Source E the USSR is trying to stir up Communist parties all over Europe to fight for Communist control. It knows that countries that take Marshall Aid will be more likely to be on America's side than on Russia"s. So this source cannot be trusted because it is trying to stir up communism in Europe hoping that more takeovers like the one in Czechoslovakia will happen.

5 Study Source F and all the other sources. How far do the other sources support the claim made in Source F that the Marshall Plan was introduced to protect democratic countries from Communism? Explain your answer. Make sure you use your own knowledge to interpret and evaluate the sources. **(8)**

Examiner's tip The obvious way to answer this question is to write a short section about each source saying whether or not it supports the claim made by Source F. This would gain you reasonable marks but the examiner is also looking for you to group the sources into two groups – those which support the claim and those which do not. You also need to decide whether or not the sources can be trusted. It is no good using a source to support the claim if the source is totally unreliable. You

Answers to mock examination paper

Answer	Mark

> need to go through all the sources and make a rough note of those which support the claim and those which do not. Then explain how the first group of sources support the claim. Don't forget to mention whether or not the sources can be trusted and remember that some sources (like Source A) might belong in both groups. Do the same with the second group of sources. You then need to come to an overall conclusion. On balance, how far do the sources support the claim? Do not worry if do you do not use every single source. Of course, you must use most of them, but what is far more important is how you use them. The answer which follows will show you how to answer this type of question.

Source A supports this claim. It explains how President Truman thought that the way to protect countries from Communism was to help them recover from war. He believed that Communism spread when people were poor and suffering. Most of Europe was devastated by the war and the winter of 1947 was a very bad one. If nothing was done the Communists might take over. The Marshall Plan was designed to rebuild Europe's prosperity so that Communism would not spread. He had seen what had happened in countries like Hungary and wanted to make sure that other countries stayed democratic. Source C also supports this view as it shows that America did not use the Marshall Plan to benefit itself but was being generous simply to help other countries. This source is reliable because it was drawn by someone who was criticising the Marshall Plan but still showed that it was to help other countries. Most of the other sources disagree with the statement. This is partly because many of them are Russian. The USSR would be criticising the Marshall Plan because it wanted to control Europe and turn it Communist but could see that the Marshall Plan might stop this happening. So the Russian sources about the Marshall Plan cannot entirely be trusted. However, there are other sources like Source A which are not Russian which do suggest that America might be using the Plan out of self interest. This is supported by Source B which suggests that America is using Marshall Aid to gain control of Europe and to create markets for American industry. This is supported by Source A. Sources D and E also disagree with the claim made in Source F. They say that the Marshall Plan is merely another version of the Truman Doctrine. This was a promise by Truman to support any countries which were being threatened by Communism. For example, the USA paid for troops to fight Communists in Greece. The USSR claims that the US is using both The Truman Doctrine and the Marshall Plan to gain control of Europe. Most of the sources disagree with the American claim in Source F and claim instead that America was trying to control Europe and take away its freedoms. However most of these sources are from the USSR and are political propaganda from the time of the Cold War and so cannot be trusted.